Managing Difficult Convers

This book is clear, easy to navigate everyone will relate to. It addresses issue̶ ......̶ people's experience of the workplace and will help to build more effective working relationships, which are fundamental to service delivery in any organisation.

Jan Barker, Learning and Development Officer, Birmingham City Council

Managing difficult conversations dealing with differences in opinion at work is a universal concern. More than 10 years ago Mel Myers introduced managers at Delcam to a reflective approach to dealing with issues in response to our problems in managing change in a growing organisation. Together we learnt the value of taking an open approach to discussions, recognising the need to promote partnership and exchange of all relevant information. We gained an understanding that we should question assumptions about colleagues' reaction when formulating our response. We found that this considered approach brought genuine benefits in supporting change with less stress. These concepts helped us maintain the open culture that is essential in a growing young company.

In this book Sue Clark and Mel Myers provide an excellent insight into the problems of having difficult conversations and using a reflective approach to manage these successfully. The annotated examples are a particularly helpful aid to understanding. Readers should keep this book close to hand to help find guidance for a forthcoming difficult discussion and to help reflect on and learn from the experience of a tough episode at work.

Ed Lambourne, Technical Director of Delcam plc

This book addresses in a practical and helpful way a set of techniques designed to make various difficult conversations not only easier but also developmental and helpful. A more open-to-learning approach emphasises that whilst nobody would claim such conversations could be made easy they can often be much better. There is a lot of practical advice and some theory to help us do a better job in a critical area of effective management.

Robin Wensley, Professor of Policy and Marketing, Director of ESRC/EPSRC AIM Research Initiative, Warwick Business School, University of Warwick

For a complete list of Management Books 2000 titles
visit our website on http://www.mb2000.com

MANAGING DIFFICULT CONVERSATIONS AT WORK

Sue Clark &
Mel Myers

2000

First published in 2007 by Management Books 2000 Ltd
Forge House, Limes Road
Kemble, Cirencester
Gloucestershire, GL7 6AD, UK
Tel: 0044 (0) 1285 771441
Fax: 0044 (0) 1285 771055
Email: info@mb2000.com
Web: www.mb2000.com

Printed and bound in Great Britain by 4edge Ltd of Hockley, Essex – www.4edge.co.uk

British Library Cataloguing in Publication Data is available

ISBN 9781852525408

Acknowledgments

We are indebted to Michael Absolum (now Principal Consultant, Evaluation Associates, Auckland) for introducing us to the work of Chris Argyris and for inspiring us with the ideas that have, twenty years later, led us to write this book. We would like to thank Jan Barker (Learning and Development Officer, Birmingham City Council) for providing us with many training opportunities for testing our developing ideas and for her generous support and encouragement. Our thanks go to the many practitioners who, through their participation in our workshops over the years, have provided us with the raw material of numerous difficult conversations and worked with us in analysing and improving on them. Our learning from these practitioners has been of great value. We are grateful to Viviane Robinson (Professor in the School of Education, University of Auckland) and Michael Absolum for giving us their permission to use a conversation from their training video 'Tackling Tough Issues' in Chapter 10.

We owe a debt of gratitude to both David Clark (Honorary lecturer, University of Birmingham) and Angela Myers (Education Consultant). To David, for his advice at the initial draft stage of the book, and for his helpful and practical editorial suggestions in the final stages of the project. To Angela, first for ongoing, critical discussion, throughout the writing of the book, based on her knowledge of the different theories that underlie it; second for trialling many of our ideas as part of her work as a trainer and consultant in FE.

We also want to thank the following practitioners who commented on various parts of the book during its development: Louise Lipman, Ruth Myers, Carolyn Pickering, Robin Wensley and Sue Wensley. We wish particularly to thank Alan Chapman and Brenda Chapman who read the complete final draft of the book and offered many helpful comments. Our thanks also go to James Alexander and Nick Dale-Harris at Management Books 2000, for making the publication of this book possible.

Our families have lived with our writing of this book for what seems a very long time. We are most grateful to them for their patience and unfailing encouragement. Finally, as joint authors, we would like to acknowledge one another's contribution to completing the project, in spite of many ups and downs and 'difficult conversations' along the way. It is our firm belief that our joint authorship has been made possible only through a shared commitment to the principles and practice of the open-to-learning model set out in this book.

Contents

Introduction

What this book is about

This book is about the difficult conversations that we have in the workplace and the range of problems that these can create, both for us as individuals and for the people with whom we work and interact. These problems include feelings of stress, anger, resentment, embarrassment, being devalued, a sense of powerlessness to affect outcomes, and impaired working relationships.

The book is designed to offer practical help in managing difficult conversations in a way that enables us to avoid such problems. We have three main aims. First, we wish to make available the findings from our own work, and those of related studies, through two models of conversation: the closed-to-learning model and the open-to learning model. Second, to provide a practical means by which, using the closed-to-learning model, we can identify aspects of our own thinking and words that contribute to making conversations difficult. The third aim is to offer a clear and usable framework – the open-to-learning model – through which we will be able to manage conversations that we find difficult in a new and effective way.

Our studies, and our own consultancy, coaching and training work with practitioners, tell us that difficult conversations are the norm in the workplace. We also know, from the same sources, that most of the suggested approaches to managing these effectively do not work, whether these are based on received wisdom, on exhaustive lists of different categories of 'difficult people' and the myriad different ways to treat them, or on ideas that are hard to make use of because they are not made clear and explicit.

Rather than dealing with the problem of difficult conversations as if the cause were to be found 'out there' with other people (managers, staff, colleagues …our clients), this book focuses on ways in which we can change *our* approach – improve our own personal, professional effectiveness in dealing with such conversations. This is not to suggest that we are uniquely responsible for the difficulties we encounter. Rather, it is a pragmatic recognition that it is more within our power to change our own approach than it is to change other people's, and that we can affect other people's behaviour indirectly, yet effectively, as a result of changing the way that we ourselves behave.

We recognise that to change the acquired, and usually quite automatic, habits of a lifetime requires hard work, understanding and skill. This is no mean task. But our experience convinces us that the benefits to be obtained by acquiring such insights and skills far outweigh the commitment and time needed to master them.

Who the book is for

This book is written by practitioners for practitioners. We believe that the insights and skills described here will be useful to any practitioner seeking to handle difficult conversations more effectively, whether at work or anywhere else. While we are primarily writing for practitioners in general, we also outline below three specific groups who, we believe, will find this book of particular interest and value.

Managers

Managers, as part of their responsibilities, typically have to deal with 'people problems' that undermine effectiveness and morale, create stress and are hard to resolve. Such situations frequently involve them in having to handle difficult conversations. Managers will find the insights and skills we offer here of considerable help in enabling them to develop more effective ways of dealing with these kinds of conversation.

Managers who have responsibility for managing change within their organization frequently find themselves in situations where resistance to change, in all its forms, gives rise to conversations that are difficult to handle. They will find the principles and skills we offer very useful in such situations.

Those working directly with clients, patients or customers

Practitioners such as social workers and probation officers, doctors and therapists and those in marketing and sales become involved, from time to time, in difficult conversations with those who use their services. When this happens, practitioners may find it difficult to fulfil their responsibilities whilst, at the same time, maintaining good working relationships with their clients, patients or customers. This book will help them achieve that aim.

Those who teach interpersonal skills

This book is a resource for those who lead courses that have a high interpersonal skills component, such as courses for social workers, human resources managers, counsellors and psychologists. The book will provide course leaders with a useful model for improving interpersonal skills, and also exercises that will enable their students to work independently.

Why we have written the book

Over the past twenty years, we have been involved – through courses, coaching and consultancy – in helping over 400 practitioners learn how to handle difficult conversations in ways that are effective for themselves and their colleagues in their various roles in the work situation. During this time, the practitioners we have worked with have asked us for reading material that would help them develop further the insights and skills that they have acquired. As a result, we produced a short handbook that could be a resource for this purpose. However, in order to assist those who wanted to continue the learning process in a more independent way, we felt the need to develop this handbook into a more comprehensive description of the two key models of conversation that we have developed and on which our work is based. We also wanted to build into it exercises similar to those offered to the practitioners with whom we have worked directly, to give readers the opportunity to gain the same practical skills.

We approach the problem of difficult conversations as psychologists with a particular perspective. In this respect, we have been greatly influenced by the work of Argyris and Schon (1974) (see Appendix A for further details of the main sources of the ideas set out in this book). However, their published work concentrates on their research and theoretical ideas, rather than addressing directly the practical needs of those who want to learn new skills. We believe that this book, building on the work of Argyris and Schon, will help to address these practical needs more directly.

The book aims to:

- enable practitioners to identify and deal with the, normally hidden, ways of thinking that lie at the heart of difficult conversations in the workplace.

- provide a comprehensive, effective and yet easy-to-remember approach to managing difficult conversations at work, based on our own findings and the work of Argyris and Schon.

- enable and encourage practitioners to be their own action researchers so that they are in a position to engage in an ongoing process of improving their skills in handling difficult conversations.

How the book is set out

Note on terminology

The terms 'the closed approach' or 'closed conversation' refer to the conversational approach based on the closed-to-learning model, while the terms 'the open approach' or 'open conversation' refer to the conversational approach based on the open-to-learning model.

We use the words 'closed' and 'open' as abbreviated forms of the terms 'closed-to-learning' and 'open-to-learning'.

There is a Glossary on page 253 where we define a number of other terms used in the book.

Book outline

Part One describes the problem of difficult conversations at work and sets the scene for a later and more detailed treatment of closed and open conversation:

> *Chapter 1* describes the universal nature of difficult conversations in the workplace. We look at the recurring features of these kinds of conversation and the negative feelings they can produce. We then identify ten of the most common types of difficult conversation. Each difficulty is illustrated by a number of workplace examples. We end the chapter by considering some of the adverse outcomes of such conversations.
>
> In *Chapter 2* we introduce the main theoretical ideas on which the book is based. We compare two approaches to managing difficult conversations, the closed-to-learning approach and the open-to-learning approach.
>
> We note that beneficial outcomes are most likely to be achieved if

we take an open-to-learning approach and make difficulties discussable. In practice, however, this can be very hard to achieve because we are typically unable to take into account the thinking that lies behind the words we use.

We identify three key aspects of our thinking, relevant to the handling of difficult conversations: our assumptions, our approach to partnership with the other person and the information we believe needs to be exchanged. We describe how we deal with these aspects of our thinking when we are in closed or open mode. We also outline the forms of words to which our closed or open-to-learning thinking gives rise.

We indicate that the closed and open approaches are based on two models, the closed-to-learning model and the open-to-learning model. We suggest that an approach based on the closed-to-learning model prevents us from making difficulties discussable and leads to adverse outcomes. An approach based on the open-to-learning model, on the other hand, enables us to make difficulties discussable and achieve beneficial outcomes.

Finally, we take an initial look at what is required to move from a closed to an open approach when managing difficult conversations.

Part Two consists of a more detailed description of the closed-to-learning approach.

Chapter 3 explores the first part of the closed model – the characteristics that make our thinking closed-to-learning. We show how such habitually closed thinking prevents us from handling difficult conversations effectively.

Chapter 4 looks at the second part of the closed model – the closed forms of words that we find ourselves employing when our thinking remains closed-to learning. We explain how these closed forms of words make our conversations ineffective.

In *Chapter 5* we give examples of an ineffective, closed approach to each of the ten common types of difficult conversation set out in Chapter 1. In each case we include the main actor's thoughts as well as their words. We show, through annotations, how an approach informed by the closed-to-learning model makes our approach to difficult conversations ineffective.

In *Part Three* we present a more detailed description of the open-to-learning approach.

Chapter 6 sets out the first part of the open-to-learning model – the principles of open-to-learning thinking. We show how this kind of thinking enables us to handle difficult conversations effectively.

Chapter 7 explores the second part of the open model – the open forms of words we need to use in order to reflect the principles of open thinking described in Chapter 6. We show some of the beneficial effects of open forms of words on our difficult conversations.

Chapter 8 tackles the critical issue of how we can move from a closed to an open approach in handling difficult conversations at work. We stress the importance of being alert to negative feelings, and of using these as cues to making our conversational approach more open.

In *Chapter 9* we show an effective, open approach to the ten examples of difficult conversations first given, in their closed versions, in Chapter 5. We again include the main actor's thoughts as well as their words. We show, through annotations, how an approach informed by the open-to-learning model makes the way we handle the conversation effective.

In *Chapter 10* we explore how the open-to-learning model can be used effectively in an extended conversation that produces a number of difficulties as it progresses.

Part Four

Chapter 11 examines how closed interpretations of organisational values create pressures to manage difficult conversations in counter-productive ways. We stress the benefits of open conversation in enabling us to overcome these pressures. We highlight the benefits to the organization and its members when managers are able to put open interpretations of organizational values into practice.

The **Conclusion** highlights the need for practitioners to make the open-to-learning approach to difficult conversations part of their professional development.

~~~~~~~~~~~~

Practical exercises to familiarise the reader with the closed-to-learning and open-to-learning approaches to difficult conversations and to help the reader to convert their understanding of principles into practical skills, are provided at the end of Chapters 1, 2, 3, 4, 6, 7, 8 and 10, and in Chapter 11. The exercises are intended to give practice in applying the main concepts that have been covered in each chapter. They will be particularly useful if combined with a study of the ten annotated conversations (Chapter 5 for the closed versions of the conversations and Chapter 9 for the open versions).

There are two **Appendices**. *Appendix A* indicates how the book is grounded in our work with practitioners, and provides brief information about the work of the authors who have influenced us. *Appendix B* provides guidance for the Key Exercise that runs throughout the book.

Ways to use the book

The book has been written so that each chapter builds on and helps to fill out those that have gone before. This will enable the reader to acquire the insights needed to manage difficult conversations effectively, while facility with the related skills can be gained if the exercises at the end of each chapter are undertaken.

However, we recognise that people learn in very different ways and that not everyone will want to read the book from cover to cover. We, therefore, offer a number of alternative suggestions for ways in which the book might be used.

- If you would like to check out quickly whether the book deals with the sort of difficult conversations you experience at work, turn to Chapter 1. There we list ten common types of difficult conversation, giving examples from the workplace. We explore further examples, in detail, in Chapters 5 and 9.

- If you would like an overview of the book's main learning points, read the 'Learning points' sections at the beginning of each chapter.

- If you want a brief outline of the closed and open-to-learning conversational models, turn to Chapter 2 where we set out the main components of each model.

- If you prefer to begin with practical situations, then turn to the annotated examples of the ten common types of difficulty that practitioners find themselves facing in conversations at work. We allocate a considerable amount of space to these as they exemplify the closed and open conversational approaches in practice. Examples of the closed approach are to be found in Chapter 5 and of the open approach in Chapter 9.

If you are interested in one particular type of difficulty, you can follow how the closed and open approaches deal with this difficulty by reading the two versions of the conversation concerned, together with their annotations, in Chapters 5 and 9.

- If you are a manager, you may find Chapter 11 a good place to start. This deals with organizational values and the closed or open ways in which these values can be interpreted and acted upon. The chapter highlights how important it is for everyone working in an organization that managers are able to put open interpretations of organizational values into practice.

- Finally, if you are interested in the sources and more general theoretical underpinnings of our approach to handling difficult conversations, Appendix A provides a brief account of our own work and of the main authors who have influenced us.

Information on ways of supplementing your reading of the book with personal instruction and practice can be found at the website www.reflectiveprocess.co.uk

The authors would be pleased to receive comment and feedback on the book via otl@reflectiveprocess.co.uk.

PART ONE

The Problem and Approaches To It

1

Difficult Conversations in the Workplace

Learning points

Difficult conversations are a universal problem.

Their difficulty is evident in a number of recurring features.

They are almost always associated with negative feelings.

Ten types of difficult conversation are particularly common.

Our difficult conversations are likely to have adverse effects on us and on our working relationships with others.

It is possible to improve our own skills in managing the difficult conversations in which we are inevitably involved.

~~~~~~~~~~~~~~~~~~~

Through a number of exercises we invite you to relate the ten types of difficult conversation to your own experience.

A universal problem

Difficult conversations, and the discomfort they bring to our working lives, are part of everyone's experience. In conducting professional development programmes over the last twenty years, we have been involved in dealing with the difficult conversations experienced by hundreds of practitioners at work. All the practitioners with whom we have worked have readily recalled conversations with colleagues or clients that they have found difficult to manage, that have raised negative feelings and that have had a damaging effect on their working relationships.

Some of these conversations were informal; others took place in the context of more formal meetings to do with such tasks as employee selection, monitoring performance, or dealing with absence. As well as difficult conversations occurring in face-to-face meetings, they also happened when practitioners were involved in phone conversations or exchanging emails.

All the practitioners we worked with reported that difficult conversations occurred frequently in their working lives. This was regardless of their level of training (some had undergone courses in people management and human relationships), their expertise and experience, their level of seniority in their organisation, and whether the organisation was a private, public or voluntary body.

Sometimes the problems the practitioners reported recurred with particular people or in specific situations. They also occurred with a wide range of people – colleagues, managers, those they themselves managed, customers and clients. Even practitioners who were in the full-time business of using 'people skills' – social workers, health professionals, psychologists, for example – frequently experienced conversations that 'went wrong'.

These difficult conversations seemed to occur despite people's best intentions. After all, most of us do not want our conversations to create negative feelings or uneasy relationships. On the contrary, what we would like is to have conversations that deal effectively with whatever the issue may be, while at the same time maintaining good working relationships with all involved.

The problem is that in trying to achieve one beneficial outcome, we very often do so at the expense of another. For example, because we want to maintain a good relationship with someone we manage, we may fail to comment on their unacceptable work. The result is that their performance does not improve. Conversely, we may say what we feel we want or need to say, but provoke hostility in the process.

Many practitioners who believe that they possess good interpersonal skills are often baffled by why their conversations go wrong. They may try to make sense of what has happened by blaming the other person or the organisation and its policies or structures. Other practitioners may be well aware that their own skills do not enable them to cope with difficult conversations, yet do not know how to improve their performance. Our work suggests that many people come to terms with the problem of difficult conversations by regarding them as an inevitable part of their working day – 'life is like that'.

What we mean by difficult conversations

By 'difficult conversations' we mean conversations that are hard to handle. They might be conversations that touch on sensitive issues; conversations where conflict occurs; conversations that make us uncomfortable; conversations with people we find it hard to get on with; or conversations that we are not looking forward to having and would sooner avoid.

When we asked the practitioners on our courses what made a conversation difficult, their answers focused on 'recurring features' and 'negative feelings'. Through discussion with them we were able to relate these features and feelings to ten common 'types of difficulty'. These features, feelings and types of difficulty are shown in Figure 1.1. We say more about them below.

Recurring features

Difficult conversations at work reveal a number of recurring features that make them hard to manage:

Intractability. Problems seem intractable because they have a long history. Just about everything has been tried and failed in an effort to resolve them. In these situations people enter the conversation with a great deal of baggage from the past which they find almost impossible to put to one side.

Taboo. The issues concerned seem so delicate or sensitive that it is impossible to mention them, let alone discuss them in any open and objective way.

Threat. People feel threatened, harassed or bullied by criticism of their behaviour, competence or judgement.

Aggression. Opinions are put forward and judgements made in an aggressive or dogmatic way. Alternatives to the point of view being expressed are dismissed with no genuine consideration of their merits.

Evasion. People employ very effective and socially acceptable techniques to evade or deny the discussion of difficult issues. In doing so, they also evade accountability.

Subversion. Describes a situation where, for whatever reason, participants seek to subvert or disrupt meetings, or to avoid difficulties being discussed.

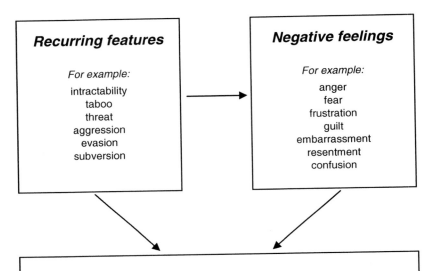

Recurring features

For example:

intractability
taboo
threat
aggression
evasion
subversion

Negative feelings

For example:

anger
fear
frustration
guilt
embarrassment
resentment
confusion

Ten common types of difficulty

1. Saying something critical to another person.

2. Communicating unwelcome information that we are obliged to convey.

3. Saying something we think will go against group consensus.

4. Retrieving a setback in an interpersonal relationship.

5. Engaging with someone who will not discuss things with us.

6. Dealing with a conflict of loyalties .

7. Coping with being criticized.

8. Responding to non-verbal behaviour that bothers us.

9. Responding to pressure to go beyond what we feel comfortable with.

10. Handling a conflict of views between ourselves and another person.

Figure 1.1 Ways in which practitioners describe what makes a conversation difficult

Negative feelings

As indicated in Figure 1.1, the recurring features of difficult conversations invariably give rise to negative feelings, such as anger, fear or frustration.

When asked about their experience of difficult conversations, practitioners find it quite easy to recall the negative feelings associated with them. Sometimes these feelings are so strong that even recalling the conversation can bring them flooding back in a way that is overwhelming and that can be disturbing. At other times people report a less vivid but enduring feeling that a conversation has 'gone wrong' in some way.

Very often negative feelings arise before a conversation even takes place. People describe as difficult those conversations that they have found themselves approaching with apprehension or that, out of anxiety, they have tried to avoid altogether. For example, they may have found themselves putting off an awkward phone call or ignoring the need to speak to someone with whom they do not get on very well.

Ten common types of difficult conversation at work

In Figure 1.1 we give examples of the ten most common types of difficult conversation reported by over 400 practitioners who have attended our workshops. Each of the conversations described by the practitioners was unique in terms of the people involved and the problems it dealt with. However, our findings have been that these ten common types of difficult conversation encompass most of the problems that people encountered

We list the ten types of difficult conversation below, together with examples of contexts in which they might be encountered.

1. Saying something critical

- Giving negative feedback to a member of staff on their performance.
- Handling a colleague who has not done what they said they would do.
- Telling our senior manager that we disagree with their policy.

2. Communicating unwelcome information that we are obliged to convey

- Telling someone that they are going to be relocated.
- Informing a project manager about the cancellation of their project.
- Telling a client that we are going to have to reduce our level of service.

3. Saying something we think will go against group consensus

- Putting forward a point of view that goes against the feeling of the meeting.
- Speaking up for a colleague who we believe is being wrongly criticised.
- Making it clear when we do not go along with a piece of gossip.

4. Retrieving a setback in an interpersonal relationship

- Dealing with the feeling that we have been unreasonably impatient with someone.
- Dealing with having made a bad decision that has adversely affected a colleague.
- Dealing with a feeling of having been hurt by a colleague.

5. Engaging with someone who refuses to discuss things with us

- Dealing with someone who responds jokingly to our attempts to have a serious conversation.
- Dealing with someone who dismisses our concerns.
- Getting our line manager to hear that we are saying 'No' to extra work.

6. Dealing with a conflict of loyalties

- Dealing with a request for a decision that would involve bypassing officially agreed channels of decision-making.
- Handling a member of staff's complaints about another member of staff.
- Feeling caught between the conflicting demands of different managers.

7. Coping with being criticised

- Responding to someone junior to us who questions our professional judgement.
- Responding to negative feedback on some aspect of our performance.
- Responding to a member of the public who complains about the way we have handled their problem.

8. Responding to non-verbal behaviour that bothers us

- Handling a situation where the person we are speaking to starts to look anxious.
- Dealing with a colleague who carries on working while we are trying to have a serious conversation.
- Responding to a manager who speaks to us in a dismissive tone of voice.

9. Responding to pressure to go beyond what we feel comfortable with

- Responding to pressure to go beyond our competence.
- Handling unwelcome pressure to give immediate advice.
- Coping with pressure to give a simple answer to a complex problem.

10. Handling a conflict of views between ourselves and another person

- Dealing with a disagreement about who should take on a particular responsibility.
- Handling a conflict of views about the best method to use.
- Handling a disagreement with a colleague about priorities.

In Chapters 5 and 9 respectively we use these ten types of difficult conversation to illustrate two different ways of dealing with the difficulties they present, using the closed-to-learning and open-to-learning approaches. [If any particular type of difficulty interests you, this can be followed through via these chapters.]

Adverse outcomes of difficult conversations at work

Difficult conversations can have serious adverse outcomes. For the individuals involved in a difficult conversation, strong negative feelings can lead to a high degree of personal stress. This can impair people's sense of well-being, learning and development. Even difficulties that may at the time appear trivial, cumulatively can bring about feelings of anxiety and powerlessness and impair our self-confidence. It is important to recognise that our difficult conversations are not merely a background irritant to be endured. They can be a very serious problem and adversely affect practitioners, whatever their level of skill, experience or seniority.

Difficult conversations are also likely to have adverse outcomes that reach well beyond any one individual. For example, where difficult conversations lead to arguments and stand-offs, they can have a negative effect on people's ability to work together and, hence, on the life and work of their organisation. Further examples of the likely adverse outcomes on the life and work of organisations, of difficult conversations that are mishandled, can be found in Chapter 5: inadequate or poorly managed feedback on job competencies can result in organisations continuing to carry weaknesses that have not been addressed; problems that are not aired or that are not addressed effectively, can lead to such adverse outcomes as continuing tensions or rivalries between people who have to work together, burn-out, reduced standards of work and inefficiency.

When managers handle difficult conversations badly the result can be reduced confidence in management and a correspondingly reduced commitment to the organisation. The research carried out by Argyris (1990) reveals strong links between the effectiveness of individuals in addressing work-related difficulties and the capacity of their organisations to learn and change.

However we know, from our extensive experience of using the approach taken in this book with practitioners, as well as from the literature, that it is possible for people to improve their skills in managing the difficult conversations in which they are inevitably concerned. The exercises below offer a first step in this process.

Exercises to help you relate the ten types of difficult conversation to your own experience

- We invite you to identify with the problem of difficult conversations at work by reading through the ten types of difficulty listed on page 25. Recall any occasions when you have been involved in one or more of these types of difficulty. As you go through the list, indicate in the margin how often this has happened in your working life: never (N) – sometimes (S) – frequently (F). You may find the bulleted examples of each of these types of difficult conversation useful as prompts.

- For one day, keep a record of any difficult conversations at work in which you are involved. If possible, make a note of these immediately after they occur. Try to relate these to the ten types of difficulty we have listed.

- Although the practitioners we worked with all recognised that they experienced difficult conversations, occasionally they had difficulties recalling them. If this is a problem for you, an alternative way of identifying some of your own difficult conversations at work is to carry out this reminiscence exercise. Recall a recent day at work and, starting from the time you arrived, work through the following four stages, illustrated in the Figure 1.2 below. In Stage 4, try to relate any difficult conversations you had to the ten types of difficulty we have described in this chapter.

Stage 1: Recall any activities during the day which involved you in interaction with other people – face-to-face or otherwise.

Stage 2: Add details of any specific conversation you remember.

Stage 3: Try and recall if you experienced any negative feeling in connection with a particular conversation, and exactly what gave rise to it.

Stage 4: Try and relate any such difficult conversation to the ten types of difficulty described in this chapter.

Stage 1	Stage 2	Stage 3	Stage 4
Activity involving interaction with others	*Any specific conversation(s) that were part of the activity*	*Any negative feelings and what gave rise to them*	*Possible relation to one of the ten types of difficulty*
Administration	Dealt with mail, email, phone messages	Shocked at suggestion that my email omitted crucial details	Coping with being criticised (Type of difficulty 7)
Met new colleagues	Gave advice as requested by line manager	Taken aback by new colleague's cold response to my advice	Retrieving a setback in an interpersonal relationship (Type of difficulty 4)
Staff meeting	Gave briefing for coming week	Annoyed by bored expression of junior colleague	Responding to non-verbal behaviour that bothers us (Type of difficulty 8)
Visits to clients	Checked agreements going to plan	No negative feelings	N/A

Figure 1.2 Example of a completed reminiscence exercise

2

Closed and Open Approaches to Managing Difficult Conversations

Learning points

To manage difficult conversations effectively, difficulties must be made discussable.

In practice this can be extremely difficult.

This is because our approach to difficult conversations is typically based on the closed-to-learning model.

In order to be able to make difficulties discussable and handle them effectively we need to employ an alternative approach – one based on the open-to-learning model.

The closed-to-learning and open-to-learning models each describe three aspects of our thinking and two associated forms of words.

It is possible to move from a closed to an open approach to difficult conversations.

~~~~~~~~~~~~~~~

We invite you to take the first step in the Key Exercise that, chapter by chapter, will enable you to identify any closed-to-learning features in your own approach to a difficult conversation and to try out an alternative, open-to-learning approach.

</div>

The need to make difficulties discussable

In order to improve our handling of difficult conversations at work, we need to be able to make difficulties discussable[1]. By 'discussable' we mean that

---
[1] We came across the word 'discussable' in Argyris (1982).

concerns can be raised and talked about in a way that is acceptable to both parties. From analysing the difficult conversations presented by the practitioners on our courses (Chapter 1), we have found that the difficulties they experience are very seldom made discussable. Issues of concern to one or other of the parties to the conversation are either not mentioned, or, if they are, the two parties find themselves unable to discuss them in a way that is acceptable to them both. This tends to result in adverse outcomes such as: entrenchment in old views and prejudices, feelings of powerlessness, defensiveness, impaired working relationships with colleagues and the failure to resolve important work issues. Our experience is that if we are able to make difficulties discussable, there is every chance that a jointly acceptable way forward will be found. The management of difficult conversations at work will then lead to beneficial outcomes both for ourselves and for our colleagues. Such outcomes will include feelings of increased professional competence, the promotion of good working relationships, the resolution of important work issues and improved morale.

When difficulties are not made discussable and there are adverse outcomes, we call such conversations 'ineffective'. We call conversations where difficulties are made discussable and where there are beneficial outcomes 'effective conversations'.

Given the challenges posed by difficult conversations, how, in practice, can we make difficulties discussable and thus manage difficult conversations effectively?

It is the way we *think* that determines how effectively we manage difficult conversations

The work of Argyris and Schon (1974), together with our own observations, has led us to the conclusion that we are unable to handle difficult conversations at work effectively because of the way we *think*.

Different ways of thinking produce different forms of words. It is the way we think and the forms of words that follow from such thinking that make difficulties discussable or not, and thus make our handling of difficult conversations effective or ineffective.

In our workshops, we asked practitioners to identify a conversation at work in which they had been involved and which left them with negative feelings. We asked them to record not only what both parties said, but also their own thinking as the conversation progressed. From several hundred such scripted conversations and from the work of Argyris (1974) and Absolum (1985), we abstracted three key aspects of our thinking that have direct relevance to the way we manage difficult conversations. These three aspects of our thinking are: the way we handle our assumptions; the extent to which we regard the conversation as a partnership; and how we approach the exchange of information.

In the Introduction we mentioned two modes of thinking: *closed-to-learning* and *open-to-learning*. We now define these in terms of the way that we deal with the three key aspects of our thinking: *assumptions*, *partnership* and *information exchange*, as summarised in Figure 2.1.

Key aspects of our thinking	When we are in closed-to-learning mode	When we are in open-to-learning mode
Assumptions	We do not question our assumptions	We question any relevant assumptions
Partnership	We do not promote partnership	We promote partnership
Information	We do not promote the exchange of all relevant information	We promote the exchange of all relevant information

Figure 2.1 How we deal with the key aspects of our thinking when we are in closed-to-learning and open-to-learning mode

In the following sections we unpack Figure 2.1 and make clear, for each key aspect in turn, the main differences in the way that we deal with that aspect of our thinking when we are in closed and when we are in open mode.

How we deal with our assumptions

The aspect of our thinking that is the most critical for the management of difficult conversations concerns the assumptions we make.

By 'assumptions' we mean any belief, theory or inference that we 'take as being true for the purpose of argument or action' (*Concise Oxford Dictionary*, 1981). Assumptions play a very important role in our thinking. They reflect our personal views about how things are, and thus the sense we make of our own and other people's behaviour. Any 'is' or 'isn't', 'do' or 'don't', 'will' or 'won't', 'always' or 'never' position that we adopt in the course of a conversation can be taken to represent an assumption. Our assumptions are often inter-related, sometimes in ways of which we are not aware. For example, the assumption that another person 'will react angrily to what I want to say' may be linked to the assumption that 'it is unacceptable to make people angry'.

The range of assumptions we might hold is potentially infinite. However, what is important in the context of difficult conversations is not what particular assumption we make, but the fact that we base what we say on the 'truth' of that assumption. So, in the example above, if we take as 'true' the related assumptions that 'the other person will react angrily' and that 'it is unacceptable to make people angry', we may decide not to say what we really want to say. In this way our assumptions shape our approach to difficult conversations.

When our thinking is closed-to-learning

When our thinking is closed-to-learning we fail to question our assumptions. Two features of assumptions contribute to this. First, they operate swiftly and spontaneously, in a manner that is largely beyond our conscious control. For example, if we are in conversation with someone and they glance at their watch, our assumptions about why they are doing so (for example 'they're double booked' or 'they don't like what I'm saying') are typically arrived at rapidly and without reflection. To the extent that our assumptions operate beyond our conscious control, we are unable to question them. Second, the assumptions we make can be extremely compelling. They are for us 'the truth' of the situation. To question our assumptions, therefore, is to act counter-intuitively.

Of course, any assumption we make can be either right or wrong. The problem is that if we make an assumption that is wrong and do not question it[2], the thoughts that are shaped by that assumption are highly likely to misdirect us.

Failure to question our assumptions brings about what Argyris and Schon (1974, p.19) call 'single-loop' learning. In this book, this means that if we fail to question the assumptions on which our approach to a difficult conversation is based, we close ourselves off from any thinking that lies outside the boundaries set by those assumptions. For instance, if we assume,

---

[2] See page 117 for a discussion of how we might test of an assumption.

unquestioningly, that a disagreement can only be resolved by one party giving in to the other, we fail even to consider other possible ways forward. In our terminology, we become closed-to-learning.

The types of unquestioned assumptions most likely to prevent us from handling a difficult conversation effectively are those we make about the other person or situation under discussion, and thus about how we should handle the conversation. If we do not question such assumptions, they lock us into old patterns of thought and limit what we are able to think, hear or say. They make it extremely difficult for us to take on board information that contradicts any personal 'taken-for-granted' position that we may hold. They also limit our repertoire for handling difficult conversations to one that supports and maintains our well-established patterns of thinking.

When our thinking is open-to-learning

Conversely, when our thinking is open-to-learning we *do* question our assumptions.

Questioning our assumptions brings about 'double-loop' learning (Argyris and Schon 1974, p.19). This enables us to break out of closed-to-learning ways of thinking so that we can adopt alternative and effective ways of dealing with conversational difficulties. For example, we might question the received wisdom that to admit a mistake is an indication of weakness rather than strength, and thus be free to handle a conversation in new ways. Because we are able to question our underlying assumptions and free ourselves from any constraints they might impose on our thinking, we are able to engage in the sort of learning that will enable us to handle the kind of difficulties that this book is about. In our terminology, we become open-to-learning.

How we deal with the idea of the conversation as a partnership

When our thinking is closed-to-learning

When our thinking is closed-to-learning we make little or no attempt to make the conversation a genuine partnership. Our work, and that of Argyris and Schon (1974) suggests that when we are faced with a difficult conversation, our thinking leads us to manage the conversation unilaterally rather than in partnership. For example, if we are having a conversation with someone we assume to be vulnerable in some way, we may find ourselves steering that conversation towards decisions that *we* believe to be in their best interests. We do not make sure *their* views and preferences are part of the decision-making process.

When we approach a conversation in unilateral rather than partnership mode, we reduce our access to points of view that the other person might otherwise offer and that might cause us to question our assumptions. In doing this we perpetuate our closed-to-learning thinking and so reduce our chances of dealing effectively with whatever difficulties face us in the conversation.

When our thinking is open-to-learning

Conversely, when our thinking is open-to-learning we seek to make the conversation a partnership. This encourages us to see difficulties as opportunities for joint ways forward rather than as concerns that we have to manage alone. This enables difficulties to be discussed in a way that is likely to resolve them. Each person's position becomes a source of new perspectives for the other.

How we deal with the exchange of information

A third aspect of our thinking, which is key to the way we handle difficult conversations, is how we approach the exchange of information. By information we mean not only facts, but people's views, wishes, concerns, reasoning, and disclosure of how they are feeling.

How we approach the exchange of information is closely related to the idea of partnership. Thus a condition of effective partnership is that both parties have access to all the information that is relevant to the conversation, so that a shared perspective is more likely to emerge on the topic under discussion.

When our thinking is closed-to-learning

When our thinking is closed-to-learning we approach the exchange of information by limiting it to what we consider expedient. We fail to promote the exchange of *all* the relevant information to which we or the other party in the conversation has access.

As with the absence of partnership, our unquestioned assumptions have a part to play in making it difficult to exchange relevant information. For example, if we assume it would not pay us to give all the information that is relevant to the conversation, we will be driven to offer only such information as we think will be to our advantage, or that is not to our disadvantage.

However, if we fail to promote the exchange of all relevant information, we will miss out on useful feedback that could cause us to question our assumptions. In so doing we again perpetuate our closed-to-learning stance and make it very hard to deal with difficulties effectively.

When our thinking is open-to-learning

Conversely, when our thinking is open-to-learning, we actively promote the exchange of all relevant information.

When we do our best to ensure that all the information that is relevant to both parties in the conversation is made available, we maximise the chance that difficulties will be made discussable. For example, making a difficulty explicit, and facilitating an exchange of information about how we feel, are important kinds of relevant information that may need to be exchanged.

[A more detailed discussion of closed-to-learning and open-to-learning thinking, including many examples, is provided in Chapters 3 and 6 respectively.]

The forms of words that result from our thinking

By 'forms of words' we mean the ways in which we formulate the words we use in a conversation, that result from, and express, closed or open-to-learning thinking.

Different ways of thinking produce different forms of words. In this section we make clear the link between the way we think and the forms of words which closed or open thinking makes possible.

Figure 2.2 sets out the forms of words we use when our thinking is closed-to-learning and open-to-learning.

To describe these forms of words, we make use of two terms 'advocacy' and 'inquiry'.[3] We use these concepts in the specific sense defined below. It is the closed or open nature of our advocacy and inquiry that makes difficulties discussable or non-discussable and leads to the conversation being managed effectively or ineffectively.

---

[3] Used by Argyris (1982)

Forms of words	Closed forms of words	Open forms of words
Advocacy	Closed advocacy • Advocacy is not transparent • Advocacy without inquiry	Open advocacy • Advocacy is transparent • Advocacy with inquiry[4]
Inquiry	Closed inquiry • Inquiry is not genuine • Inquiry without advocacy	Open inquiry • Inquiry is genuine • Inquiry with advocacy[4]

Figure 2.2 Closed-to-learning and open-to-learning forms of words

Advocacy

Advocacy refers to statements we make that convey information about the way we see things. Such statements give expression to our wishes, views, reasoning, feelings or concerns. Advocacy is closely linked to the third aspect of our thinking described above – the exchange of information between ourselves and the other person.

Closed advocacy

When our thinking is closed, the type of advocacy we find ourselves using in a difficult conversation will also be closed. Our statements will demonstrate either or both of the following features:

- They do not make the facts, feelings or reasoning that lie behind them clear enough to the listener to enable them to evaluate or fully understand our perspective. In this case we say that 'advocacy is not transparent'.

- They simply assert our own position. They are not accompanied by questions designed to find out the other person's response to what we say. We call this 'advocacy without inquiry'.

In both these ways closed advocacy governs the flow of information, and

---

[4] The sequencing of advocacy and inquiry was first introduced to us by Michael Absolum (1985)

limits the speaker's opportunity to learn about the other's perspective, thus severely reducing the likelihood of partnership. Assumptions remain unquestioned.

Open advocacy

Open advocacy results from thinking that is open-to-learning. It is the mirror image of closed advocacy. Statements that possess either of the following features demonstrate openness, though our approach will be most open when our advocacy has both:

- The facts, reasoning or feelings that lie behind our statements are made available to the listener so that they are in a position to evaluate what we say and understand our perspective. In this case we say that 'advocacy is transparent'.

- Our statements are accompanied by a request for feedback, a response to what we say. We describe this as 'advocacy with inquiry'.

When advocacy is open in these ways, new information can enter the conversation and change the way the participants see the situation or issues concerned. This leads to the possibility of assumptions being questioned and partnership being established.

Inquiry

Inquiry refers to questions we ask in order to discover the other person's wishes, views, reasoning, feelings or problems. Inquiry is closely linked to the second aspect of our thinking described above – the promotion of partnership.

Closed inquiry

When our thinking is closed, inquiry will also be closed. Closed inquiry takes either or both of the following forms:

- We may ask questions that are not genuine requests for information. Our checking of the other person's response may be perfunctory or routine, or our questions may be rhetorical i.e. statements in question form. In this case we say that 'inquiry is not genuine'.

- We ask questions without telling the other person why we are asking them. We call this 'inquiry without advocacy'.

Like closed advocacy, closed inquiry governs the two-way flow of information. It disadvantages the other person, who may be left uncertain how to reply. In both cases partnership is put at risk and assumptions are likely to remain unquestioned.

Open inquiry

Open inquiry expresses thinking that is open-to-learning and is the mirror image of closed inquiry. It takes either or both of the following forms:

- The questions we ask offer people a genuine choice as to how they reply (for example, they convey that a 'yes' or 'no' answer would be equally acceptable) or they may invite further discussion. In this case we say that 'inquiry is genuine'.

- When we ask a question, we make clear our reason for asking it. We call this 'inquiry with advocacy'.

Open inquiry is a powerful strategy both for turning the conversation into a partnership and for making it possible to check out our assumptions.

[A more detailed discussion of closed advocacy and closed inquiry can be found in Chapter 4. A further discussion of open advocacy and open inquiry can be found in Chapter 7.]

Two ways of approaching a difficult conversation: the closed-to-learning and open-to-learning models

Closed-to-learning thinking and closed-to-learning forms of words are components of what we call the 'closed-to-learning model'. Open-to-learning thinking and open-to-learning forms of words are the components of what we term the 'open-to-learning model'.

These two models are set out in Figure 2.3. In the closed-to-learning model we use the term 'characteristics' of closed-to-learning thinking, since this type of thinking is automatic and habitual. In the open-to-learning model we use the term 'principles' of open-to-learning thinking, since we need to be consciously aware of these guidelines and to choose to use them. The arrows in the figure indicate that open and closed thinking give rise to the closed and open forms of words. They are intended to reinforce the crucial point that the forms of words we use are a consequence of our thinking. Crucial because, as we shall see later, it is only by altering our thinking that we can change the forms of words we use, and, hence, become more effective in managing our difficult conversations.

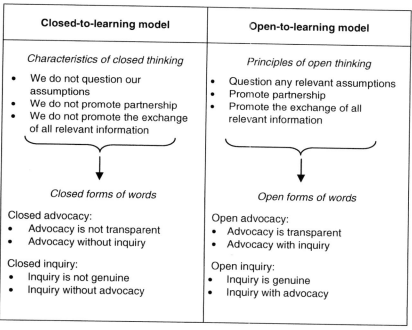

Figure 2.3 The closed-to-learning and open-to-learning models

The closed-to-learning model

The components of the closed-to-learning model (Figure 2.3) work together to make it virtually impossible for us to make difficulties discussable and to address difficult conversations effectively. Knowledge of the closed-to-learning model is essential because it offers us a means of understanding why difficult conversations are so common, yet so hard to handle. It also offers us a basis for seeing what it is that we do that makes our own conversations go wrong.

We habitually operate in closed mode

The research of Argyris and Schon suggests that most of us habitually operate in closed-to-learning mode. This becomes particularly problematic when we face a difficult conversation. Argyris and Schon (Introduction to the Classic Paperback edition of *Theory and Practice*, 1992) note that 'well over five thousand individuals...acted consistently with Model 1' (Argyris and Schon's Model 1 and Model II are the forerunners of our closed-to-learning and open-to-learning models respectively[5]). As mentioned earlier, we ourselves have identified a closed-to-learning approach in every one of the hundreds of difficult conversations which the practitioners we have worked with have contributed and which they described as ineffective.

If this approach leads to the negative feelings and adverse outcomes described in Chapter 1, why is it that so many competent practitioners continue to operate in closed-to-learning mode when handling a difficult conversation? Why do we remain trapped in habitual ways of thinking and unable to escape the self-maintaining single-loop approach that this creates? There are a number of reasons for this.

First, we do not question closed thinking because it is largely inaccessible to us. As we noted earlier in the chapter, a crucial feature of the closed-to-learning model is that the way we think, and hence our choice of words, takes place swiftly and in a manner that is largely beyond our conscious control. The sheer speed of this unconscious use of well-rehearsed patterns of thought and forms of words is one of the reasons why we are unable to take anything but our habitual approach to a difficult conversation. Under these circumstances, we are unable to gain any insight into the origins of our difficulties and are thus unable to do anything about them.

Second, we often assume that we are in open mode when we are not. We are unable to see that our own thinking has closed characteristics that are adversely affecting our ability to handle a difficult situation. The individuals cited by Argyris and Schon (1974) were able to identify closed characteristics in others, but were unable to recognise the same characteristics in themselves. Argyris and Schon describe this phenomenon as incongruence between people's 'espoused theories' and their 'theories-in-use'.

> When someone is asked how he would behave under certain circumstances, the answer he usually gives is his espoused theory of action in that situation. This is the theory of action to which he gives allegiance, and which, upon request, he communicates to others.

---

[5] See Appendix A for more information about Model I and Model II, and for some similarities and differences between these models and the closed and open-to-learning models.

However, the theory that actually governs his actions is his theory-in-use which may or may nor be compatible with his espoused theory; furthermore, the individual may or may not be aware of the incompatibility of the two theories. *(ibid.1974, pp.6-7).*

One other reason why we do not question our closed thinking is because it is usually the only approach to difficult conversations that we have in our repertoire. It is not until practitioners have learnt an open-to-learning approach that they are able to try out radically different ways of replaying their difficult conversations and handle them more effectively.

Given that our habitual mode of operating is closed-to-learning, we can describe the closed-to-learning model as 'the default mode'.

The open-to-learning model

In contrast to the automatic and habitual nature of the closed model, the open-to-learning model depends on our making conscious use of a number of factors: an awareness of the way we think; the adoption of a set of principles to guide our thinking (of which the primary one is questioning our assumptions); and the skill of ensuring that the forms of words we use reflect that thinking. These work together to make difficulties discussable and improve our management of difficult conversations.

When practitioners who attend our workshops try out the open-to-learning approach, they find that it brings many benefits. For example:

- They are more able to treat each situation on its own merits, unconstrained by previously unquestioned assumptions. This enables them to take a fresh approach that overcomes those recurring features of difficult conversations described in Chapter 1 (Figure 1.1).

- Given permission to make the conversation a partnership frees practitioners from the strain of feeling they have to act in an adversarial way. They can feel less defensive and more relaxed. As a result, new possibilities and unexpected solutions emerge to problems that previously appeared intractable.

- Once practitioners acquire the skill of being able to say what is on their minds in a way that the other person finds acceptable, they feel free to talk about difficult issues without fear of upsetting the other person and undermining working relationships.

We can be virtually certain that an approach to difficult conversations that is genuinely based on the open-to-learning model will achieve better outcomes than can ever be achieved by a closed approach. In addition, an open-to-learning approach is very likely to lead to an outcome that is negotiated by, and acceptable to, both participants.

Given the benefits of taking an open-to-learning approach to difficult conversations, what can we do to move out of closed and into open mode?

How we can move out of closed and into open mode

Moving away from a closed approach and learning to adopt an open approach to the difficult conversations we encounter at work can be extremely difficult. It involves unlearning the habits of a lifetime. It requires an awareness of any closed components in our current approach to difficult conversations, an understanding of why an open approach is so effective, the acquisition of open-to-learning skills, and a commitment to develop those skills by practising and reviewing them.

In Chapter 8 we suggest a strategy for overcoming the habitual and unconscious operation of the closed-to-learning model during a difficult conversation. Feelings of discomfort or unease alert us to the fact that we are in closed mode. These can cue us to 'think open' and remind us of the three principles and two open forms of words that lie at the heart of the open-to-learning model.

The purpose of the rest of this book is to make available the framework and practical skills to move out of closed mode and into open mode when we approach or are engaged in difficult conversations at work. This will enable us to make difficulties discussable, deal with them effectively and bring about beneficial outcomes.

In Part Two of the book we describe and discuss the closed-to-learning model in detail. We elaborate on the characteristics and closed forms of words shown in Figure 2.2, and suggest exercises for identifying these in the readers' own practice. In Part Three we then describe and discuss the open-to-learning model in order to make available the alternative approach that is needed if we are to escape our habitual ways of managing difficult conversations. We also provide exercises for practising the principles and forms of words associated with the open model.

Key exercise step 1:
Recording one of your own difficult conversations

Before moving on to the next Part of this book, we encourage you try out the first step of the exercise given in Appendix B (page 242). Its purpose is to provide you with a written sample of your own approach to a difficult conversation. This is the Key Exercise that continues throughout the book. In later steps, introduced at the end of subsequent chapters, we encourage you to build on what you have written, to analyse it in the light of the closed-to-learning approach and to re-write it in the light of the open-to-learning approach.

The two-column format for this exercise, with the writer's thoughts in one column and their words in another, was first suggested by Argyris and Schon (1974). The exercise allows us to look at a real-life conversation in slow motion and to subject it to detailed analysis. By exploring how we think and speak, we can give ourselves the critical feedback needed for reflection and learning, and for changing the way we manage our difficult conversations.

PART TWO

The Closed-to-Learning Approach

3

Three Characteristics of Closed-to-Learning Thinking

Learning points

A detailed understanding of the three characteristics of closed-to-learning thinking.

How these three characteristics keep us trapped in the type of thinking that leads to ineffectiveness in managing difficult conversations.

A framework for evaluating our own thinking in terms of the closed-to-learning model.

~~~~~~~~~~~~~~~~~~~

Through a number of exercises we invite you to explore ways in which your own thinking in a difficult conversation is closed-to-learning.

The closed-to-learning model: closed thinking

In this chapter we focus on the first part of the closed-to-learning model, the nature of closed-to-learning thinking. This is the type of thinking that our own work, and that of others (Absolum 1985, Argryis 1990, Robinson and Lai 2006), suggests leads to ineffective ways of handling difficulties and to adverse outcomes. Our main purposes in this chapter are to highlight the extent to which we ourselves typically think in closed-to-learning ways, to show how this creates problems for us when we are faced with a difficult conversation, and to provide insights into the sort of thinking that we might need to avoid or change in order to be able to handle difficult conversations effectively.

We saw, in Chapter 2, that closed-to-learning thinking has three characteristics:

Characteristic One: We do not question our assumptions.
Characteristic Two: We do not promote partnership.
Characteristic Three: We do not promote the exchange of all relevant information.

The following analysis of these three characteristics provides us with a powerful tool for understanding and evaluating our own closed thinking. When we see from this evaluation the ways in which our thinking is often closed, we are in a better to position to appreciate the need for the alternative ways of thinking that we describe in detail in Part Three.

We give a detailed coverage of the three characteristics. The reason for doing this is to make it easier to recognise closed-to-learning aspects of our thinking that we are not normally aware of, or used to looking at. These tend to occur, and affect what we say, very quickly.

Characteristic One:
We do not question our assumptions

Assumptions that we do not question form boundaries to our thinking that trap us in old habits of thought and limit what we are able to think, hear and say. This creates two serious problems. First, unquestioned assumptions make it difficult for us to take on board information that does not fit with our personal 'taken-for-granted' position. Second, if we do not question our assumptions, they limit our repertoire for handling difficult conversations to those approaches that unconsciously support and maintain our habitual, closed thinking. For both these reasons we remain closed-to-learning.

Because of these two problems, we regard Characteristic One, the failure to question our assumptions, as the most important of the three characteristics. In order to explain its effect and demonstrate its importance, we will look at each of these problems in turn.

We avoid taking on board information that does not fit with our personal 'taken-for-granted' position

When our assumptions remain unquestioned, they make it difficult for us to take on board information that conflicts with our habitual way of seeing things. There are three main ways in which we typically deal with information that does not fit with our taken-for-granted position: by screening it out; by discrediting the speaker; or by making our interpretation of the information received fit our assumptions.

We screen out information that does not fit with our assumptions

When we are exposed to information that might challenge our assumptions about the other person or about the issue under discussion, we may deal with such information by screening it out and not allowing it to register with us. The problem is that because we have screened out the very information that might lead us to change our assumptions, we remain trapped in habitual ways of thinking.

Example
We hold the unquestioned assumption that a colleague is an unimaginative person. This can lead us to screen out – fail to notice or remember – any creative ideas that the colleague may come up with.

As well as affecting our perception of an individual as in the above example, screening out is also a mechanism by which particular perceptions of others become entrenched. For example, the form of assumption we call a stereotype can cause us to notice only evidence that fits that stereotype (whether it is based on status, educational background, gender, age or race) and fail to notice evidence that contradicts it.

Example
If we hold the stereotypical assumption that elderly women drive over-cautiously, we may fail to register those occasions when a cautiously driven car is driven by someone who is not an elderly woman. We see only what we expect to see and in this way confirm and reinforce our stereotype.

We discredit the speaker

Another way of dealing with our discomfort when our assumptions are challenged, is by mentally discrediting the speaker. This makes it easier for us to dismiss what they say rather than acknowledge their point of view. The problem is that when we do this we prevent ourselves from taking on board the very information that we might need to hear in order to free up our thinking.

Example

A colleague criticises the way we are managing a project that we assume to be going well. Rather than hearing what our colleague has to say, we deal with the criticism by telling ourselves that the colleague is not competent to express an opinion. This allows us to retain our own (perhaps unfounded) confidence in our own judgement.

We make our interpretation of the information received fit with our assumptions

A third way that we deal with information that does not fit with our assumptions is to interpret it in such a way that it then fits those assumptions. This makes the information acceptable to us and avoids us having to examine the possibility that there may be other ways of seeing things.

Example

We receive a complaint about a product that we have always assumed to be excellent. In order to preserve our belief in the product, we might deal with the challenge posed by the complaint by telling ourselves that the fault is not with the product but with the customer. Thus we ensure that our interpretation of the information fits with our assumptions, but at the likely cost of making an unhelpful and inappropriate response.

The problem here is that if we regularly react to unwelcome information from others by re-interpreting what they say to fit our own assumptions, there is a serious danger that we will become out of touch and risk making ill-informed decisions. And, if people perceive us to be ignoring or manipulating their information in this way, we also increase the likelihood of our conversations with them becoming even more difficult.

Each of these three ways of dealing with information that conflicts with our assumptions prevents us from taking account of anything that might challenge those assumptions. They keep us trapped in our habitual way of seeing things.

We limit our repertoire for handling difficult conversations

Our assumptions, if unquestioned, limit our repertoire for handling difficult conversations. This is because unquestioned assumptions are strong and typically unconscious determinants of the approach we find ourselves taking. For example, if we hold the assumption that someone is 'out to get us', our approach to a conversation with that person is likely to be one of attack or defence. It does not allow us to consider the possibility of an alternative approach, such as one that is co-operative.

In routine conversations, unquestioned assumptions, and the limited approach they allow us, may not create problems. However, when we are faced with a conversation that poses difficulties, our unquestioned assumptions and the approach they determine will greatly limit our repertoire for handling these difficulties. This, in turn, makes it very unlikely that important issues will become discussable.

Example

A practitioner (**A**) is frustrated because every time he meets with his colleague (**B**) he finds himself on the listening end of a monologue and never gets the chance to put his own point of view. **A** decides to do something about it. He thinks:

'I wish **B** would stop talking. I can never get a word in edgeways. But there's no point in saying anything about it...that's just how he is. Maybe next time we have a meeting I'll start by telling him that I'm short of time... and hope he gets the message that he needs to allow time for me to have my say.'

In this example *A* makes an assumption that he does not question: 'there's no point in saying anything about it... that's just how he is'. Notice how this assumption prevents *A* from making explicit the difficulty that concerns him – *B*'s talkativeness – since to do so would contradict his assumption. As a result there is no possibility that the issue of *B*'s garrulousness can be discussed. *A*'s unquestioned assumption prevents him from considering 'saying anything about it'. Even though, on another occasion *A* may try a different strategy, his unquestioned assumption (that 'there's no point in saying anything about') will ensure that he enacts just another version of the same ineffective approach.

Whether *A*'s assumption (or any assumption we might make) is 'right' or 'wrong' is not the issue. The point is that unquestioned assumptions limit the way in which we are able to approach a difficult conversation. Nevertheless, it is important to be aware that our assumptions can be wrong. Where this is the case, such assumptions will inevitably exert a powerful negative effect on our ability to handle a difficult conversation effectively. In the example above, *A* may be quite correct in his assumption that 'there's no point in saying anything about it'. However, if his assumption is incorrect (in that *B* might actually be influenced by feedback on the problems caused by his talkativeness), **A** has lost an opportunity to bring about new learning that might improve the situation for them both.

Characteristic One is the most important of the three characteristics. By limiting what new information we are able to 'hear', Characteristic One preserves our view of the world and keeps us closed-to-learning.

Characteristic One is also responsible for limiting our repertoire for handling a difficult conversation because it paves the way for Characteristics Two and Three. In presenting Characteristics Two and Three we reflect further on this limited repertoire and show how it supports and maintains us in our closed-to-learning mode of thinking.

Characteristic Two:
We do not promote partnership

Characteristic Two describes the type of thinking in which we fail to recognise the importance of involving the other person in the management of the conversation. This type of thinking was very evident in the transcripts (over 500) of difficult conversations at work, written by practitioners on the many courses we have conducted.

Below, we examine three major ways in which we fail to promote partnership.

- We do not check out our understanding of the other person's viewpoint.
- We pursue our own agenda without reference to that of the other person.
- We decide, unilaterally, how to protect ourselves and/or the other person.

We do not check out our understanding of the other person's viewpoint

When our thinking is closed-to-learning, we often jump to our own conclusions and fail to check out the other person's viewpoint. If we misunderstand the other person's viewpoint, the discussion cannot be a partnership. This is likely to create escalating problems and difficulties that will become undiscussable. We illustrate this with reference to the way we tend to 'read' the other person's non-verbal behaviour and to guess their thoughts and feelings.

We 'read' non-verbal signs as telling us what the other person is thinking or feeling

Example
'He's frowning – that must mean that he doesn't like what I'm saying.'
[This example is taken from the closed version of Conversation 8, page 101]

Non-verbal behaviour, such as a person's posture, facial expression or tone of voice, is a common source of rapidly made assumptions. However, non-verbal behaviour may be interpreted in more than one way. The person in the above example may be frowning because they are thinking hard, or because they have a headache. When we do not question such assumptions (Characteristic One), we do not check with the other person what their non-verbal behaviour means. As a result, the responses we make may puzzle the other person, who may be unaware of their own non-verbal behaviour and/or of our interpretation of it. Thus it severely reduces any hope of making the conversation into a partnership.

We rely on guessing the other person's thoughts and feelings

Example
'I'm sure she won't mind if I leave early, so there's no need mention it now.'

If we do not check the other person's views on difficult issues that concern us, we can only guess what those views might be. The problem here is that we risk getting it wrong. It may be that 'she *will* mind if I leave early'. We may thus act (leave early) on the basis of false assumptions.

Very often, the more closely we live or work with someone, the more we believe that we know their views. This can lead us to be less careful about checking out their opinions than we would be if we were dealing with someone less familiar. If we do not explicitly check a person's position, however well we feel we know them, we run the risk of acting on a false premise and undermining any sense of partnership.

We pursue our own agenda without reference to that of the other person

We often have a clear idea of what we want out of a conversation. When our personal agenda dominates our thinking we are likely to forget, or deliberately ignore, the fact that the other person has an agenda that may not be the same as ours. If we seek to pursue our agenda without reference to theirs, any 'discussion' is unlikely to be a partnership and thus risks being ineffective in dealing with difficulties. The outcomes tend to be either non-resolution of an issue (because it is not actually raised, because the two parties cannot agree or because there is an actual argument) or a resolution that leaves one party feeling they have 'lost' and the other has 'won'. The following illustrates ways in which we pursue our own agenda.

We plan our moves as if we were playing chess

'Chess-like' thinking is when we plan our moves in order to ensure a 'win' for our own agenda. It can lead us into considerable problems if the other person fails to respond in the way that our chess-like approach predicts. Even if they do respond as predicted, our manipulation of the conversation may leave them feeling as if they are not equal partners in the conversation or lead to them feeling hostile towards us. Either way, if we are wholly directed towards our own goals, we perpetuate our own closed-to-learning thinking and work against making the difficulty discussable.

Example
'If I can get her to admit that she has completed her back-log of work, she'll find it hard to refuse when I ask her to take on something else.'

We do not take account of what the other person might think or want

Because of our pre-occupation with our own agenda, it may not occur to us, or we may not choose to check, the response of the other person to our plans. However, the other person may not see things in the way we do. If we do not acknowledge that they too may have a stake in what could be a contentious issue, we risk creating resentment and resistance.

Example
'I'll simply inform the staff that from Monday next we shall be starting afternoon sessions an hour earlier.'

We assume that it is acceptable to impose information on the other person that is relevant to our agenda but which may not be relevant to theirs

In some conversations we can find ourselves giving the other person information, regardless of whether or not they need or want to hear it. However, presenting another person with information that is relevant to our agenda but not necessarily to theirs, can come over as an imposition, particularly if we speak at length. Such behaviour militates against a shared discussion and is detrimental to making the conversation a partnership.

Example
'I'll let him know in great detail what I achieved in my last job so he will know that I'm very experienced.'

We decide, unilaterally, how to protect ourselves and/or the other person

When we are faced with a sensitive issue that we fear may upset or have an adverse effect on ourselves or the other person, we may try to protect each other without involving the other person. However, such unilateral action pre-empts the possibility of making the sensitive issue discussable. We give examples of ways in which we do this below.

We ignore our own or others' negative feelings

We try to protect ourselves and others from having to deal with negative feelings, by ignoring them.

Example
'The best thing is to act as though the argument we had this morning never happened.'
[This example is taken from the closed version of Conversation 4, page 90]

Thinking in this way prevents us from making negative feelings discussable. However when negative feelings are not made discussable they can easily surface and impact on a conversation in a destructive way. By 'leaking out' (showing themselves in body posture, tone of voice or facial expression, for example) such feelings can adversely affect those involved and threaten the good relationship we are trying to maintain.

We devise ways to stop or divert a discussion in which we are feeling uncomfortable

We may use various methods to stop or divert discussion that makes us feel uncomfortable, such as changing the topic, making a flippant remark that signals our unwillingness to pursue the issue with any seriousness, or saying something that can be interpreted as a put-down.

Example
'There's always someone who'll find something to criticise in what I do...I'll let him know that I'll be watching how *he* does!'
[*This example is taken from the closed version of Conversation 7, page 98*]

Such methods can threaten good relationships by arousing anger or resentment in the other person, while preventing real difficulties from being dealt with. They thus work against the idea of partnership.

We decide what is best for the other person without considering their real wishes

Concern about the other person's feelings or well-being can make us want to help them by taking charge or giving advice. However, people may not wish to be helped in the way we imagine. If our closed-to-learning thinking prevents us from acting in ways that do not consider the other person's real wishes, we cannot make the conversation a partnership.

Examples
'She's still not well... I'll make sure she goes home early today.'
'She's out of her depth... I'll advise her how to manage the situation.'

Characteristic Three:
We do not promote the exchange of all relevant information

Characteristic Three describes a way of thinking which prevents us promoting an exchange of all the information that is relevant to the conversation. For these purposes, 'all relevant information' includes any concerns, wishes, views, reasoning or feelings that have a direct bearing on our conversation. We also include any information that enables those involved in a conversation to judge the validity or worth of what is said.

In our courses and workshops, we asked practitioners to record a difficult conversation by writing down both the words of the conversation and their concurrent thoughts. We invariably found that their thinking revealed important information that did not appear in their words. This prevented difficulties becoming discussable and reduced the likelihood of beneficial outcomes.

Below, we look at three types of thinking that frequently prevent the exchange of all relevant information. These are:

- We regard certain problems as no-go areas for discussion.
- We take for granted that we both have all the information we need.
- We plan to communicate information 'strategically'.

We regard certain problems as no-go areas for discussion

Examples are as follows:

We avoid raising or discussing anything we think may be upsetting, embarrassing, controversial or threatening

Example
A manager is worried about telling a member of staff that he has not approved her promotion because of her poor interpersonal skills. Because of this he avoids telling her the real reason why she has not been promoted. Instead he gives her vague reassurances that 'it is just one of those things' and that she remains 'really valued'.

[This example is taken from the closed version of Conversation 1, page 79.]

Argyris describes this type of approach to anything embarrassing or threatening as a 'cover-up' (Argyris 1990). He observes that this way of handling difficulties is commonplace in working life, but that it has a profoundly negative impact on individuals and organisations.

We regard the non-discussion of such difficulties as itself undiscussable

In the exchange just described, it is unusual for the manager to ask, 'Are you satisfied with my explanation about why you have not been promoted?' Likewise, it is rare for the member of staff to say, 'I'm not happy with your explanation. I think there may be other reasons that you are not telling me about.'

Such comments, while theoretically possible, are seldom made. Hence the non-discussability of what are in reality important difficulties is itself treated as non-discussable. Both participants behave as though there were nothing going on behind the scenes. This makes it what Argyris terms 'self-sealed' from learning and change (Argyris 1990 p.30).

We take for granted that we both have all the information we need

Examples are as follows:

We do not appreciate that the other person may not know our problem (and/or that we may not know the other person's problem)

Very often we assume that the other person knows the difficulty we are experiencing, or that we know what problem they are experiencing when this is not the case. Unless there is an attempt to make the concerns and difficulties of both parties in the conversation explicit (rather than assuming they are common knowledge or simply hinting at them), they are very likely to remain undiscussed. One or both participants may feel resentful that their problem has not been appreciated or dealt with. Thus the conversation is very likely to have adverse outcomes.

> *Examples*
> 'She can see I've got a problem and yet she still expects me to...'
> 'She hasn't said anything. Therefore she can't be worried.'

We do not appreciate that the other person may be unaware of the background to what we say (or that we may be unaware of the background to what they say)

Such is our familiarity with our own background knowledge and reasoning that we may easily forget that these are not necessarily known to the other person. If we do not disclose them, the other person does not have enough information to assess the validity of what we say. This means that they will not be able to let us know if our information is wrong, out of date or incomplete, or that our reasoning is in some way faulty. There is then the risk that the discussion will be marked by misunderstandings, argument and ineffective handling of difficulties. Similar problems will arise if we remain unaware of background information relating to what the other person says that is relevant to the conversation.

> *Examples*
> 'She knows the situation...'
> 'My reasons are obvious.'

It does not occur to us to let the other person know when we have negative feelings that are relevant to the conversation

Because our feelings are obvious to us, we expect that they are obvious to the other person. Thus we see no need to communicate information about them.

Example
'He should have seen I was feeling upset.'

We may also reject the idea of communicating our feelings because of an unquestioned assumption that, within a workspace culture, negative feelings should be kept hidden. However, unless we make negative feelings explicit, they are very likely to exert a behind-the-scenes influence on the way we approach the conversation and make it less likely that difficulties will become discussable.

We plan to communicate information 'strategically'

There are times when we give or withhold relevant information in order to pursue our own agenda. Such strategic thinking can result in games-playing that militates against the disclosure of problematic issues, working in partnership and an effective way of handling difficulties. Examples are as follows:

We pick and choose what information it feels expedient to give or to withhold

Examples
'I'll warn people there are going to be some changes but I won't say what we have in mind until it's a fait accompli, in case they make a fuss.'
'If I let him know that we're discussing his proposal on Wednesday he'll want to come along. So I'll keep quiet about it.'
'I don't want him to know that I'm not sure. It might look unprofessional.'
'I won't tell any lies but I'll not say any more than I have to.'

This kind of thinking is sometimes justified by the way in which the 'social virtue' of honesty is interpreted within the workplace – for instance, as telling the truth but not the whole truth (Argyris 1990)[6]. The problem with

---

[6] See Chapter 11 for closed and open interpretations of other 'social virtues'.

this interpretation of honesty is that it works against the open exchange of all relevant information and the resolution of difficulties. As a result it severely limits the possibilities for learning and appropriate change.

In cases where we fear that what we want to say may be unwelcome to the other person, we beat about the bush or 'ease in' rather than give straight information

> *Examples*
> 'I'll start by giving her a bit of background so that when I tell her there's a problem she'll be better prepared.'
> 'If I start by asking her what she thinks, that will give me a clue as to where to pitch my own comments.'
> 'Always give the good news first.'

Because we feel anxious, we find ourselves thinking up strategies that we believe will make what we want to say more acceptable to the other person. Some of these ways of thinking may reflect the received wisdom of the workplace culture, as in the third example above ('Always give the good news first'). However, approaches that skirt sensitive issues make it hard to make difficulties discussable, not least because if the other person senses that important information is being withheld they may become anxious or angry. Such strategies are, therefore, likely to fail to reassure or protect ourselves or others.

We find ourselves planning to give information whose validity is unverifiable or that is spurious

Our unquestioned assumptions can take on the air of certainties. We can, without realising it, think of them as facts rather than beliefs. This can result in thinking that is potentially problematic, when the validity of our beliefs is unverifiable or when the beliefs themselves are spurious.

> *Examples*
> 'I'll tell them that the boss has no time for people who disagree with him.'
> 'I'll remind him that, as we all know, our clients don't really understand the regulations.'

Here, for instance, the practitioner believes that 'the boss has no time for people who disagree with him', and does not recognise this as an unverifiable personal opinion. The expression '... as we all know...' suggests a fact when it is, in reality, a spurious claim.

Unverifiable and spurious information can make the issue at stake undiscussable. It is difficult to challenge claims like ' ..as we all know' or personal beliefs presented as facts. Such statements work against reliable learning and reduce the likelihood of beneficial outcomes.

The three characteristics trap us in old habits of thought

In this chapter we have taken the first step in dealing with our difficult conversations by showing that the roots of these difficulties lie in the (closed) way that we normally think.

Because they are all features of closed-to-learning thinking, the three characteristics are necessarily inter-related. Thus, when we find a conversation hard to handle, it is likely that all three will be shaping our thinking in some way or another.

The three characteristics, acting together, cut us off from the possibility of learning and appropriate change. We cannot learn so long as our unquestioned assumptions prevent us from taking on board new information (Characteristic One), we do not try to involve the other person in managing the conversation (Characteristic Two), or we see no need to exchange all relevant information (Characteristic Three). In these ways we cut ourselves off from crucial sources of new learning.

Closed-to-learning thinking represented by these three characteristics also works against making difficulties discussable. Difficulties cannot be made explicit when unquestioned assumptions rule that out (Characteristic One). If difficulties are not made explicit, we will be unable to discuss them in partnership (Characteristic Two). Unquestioned assumptions and a lack of partnership will lead us to neglect sharing information that is relevant to resolving the difficulties (Characteristic Three).

Together the three characteristics of closed-to-learning thinking keep us within a familiar but closed world. As a result we can do nothing other than approach difficult conversations in old and well-rehearsed ways. The problem is that the approaches we habitually find ourselves using are the very ones that are ineffective and that make difficult conversations a recurring and potentially highly stressful feature of our working lives.

In the next chapter we will see how our closed thinking obliges us to use closed forms of words in our conversations and how this, in turn, makes us ineffective in dealing with the difficulties that we encounter.

Exercises to aid recognition of the three closed-to-learning characteristics in your own thinking

Characteristic One: We do not question our assumptions

- Next time you become worried about a forthcoming conversation, notice any assumptions you are making that may be contributing to your anxiety.

- Try to be aware when your assumptions prevent you from making a difficulty explicit.

- When you have conversations with colleagues, observe their gestures, facial expressions and tone of voice. Notice how rapidly you make assumptions about what they may be thinking on the basis of such non-verbal information without checking out that these assumptions are correct.

Characteristic Two: We do not promote partnership

- Notice when your approach to managing a conversation is 'chess-like' in that you privately plan your moves in order to pursue your own agenda.

- Notice when you make decisions which you believe to be in another person's best interests without consulting them.

Characteristic Three: We do not promote the exchange of all relevant information

- When you have difficult conversations notice those occasions when you decide, for whatever reason, that it would be best to withhold information that you know is relevant.

- When you are worried about how the other person may react to what you want to say notice if you 'beat about the bush' rather than giving straight, relevant information.

Key exercise step 2:

Evaluating your thoughts in terms of the closed-to-learning model

Instructions for Step 2 of the Key Exercise are to be found in Appendix B under the heading **'Evaluating your thoughts in terms of the closed-to-learning model'** (page 245). This will guide you to evaluate your thoughts in the difficult conversation you recorded in Step 1, in terms of the three characteristics of closed-to-learning thinking.

$$4$$

The Forms of Words that Result from Closed-to-Learning Thinking

Learning points

Closed thinking leads to two closed forms of words: closed advocacy and closed inquiry.

These closed forms of words make difficulties undiscussable.

~~~~~~~~~~~~~~~~~~~~~~~

Through a number of exercises we invite you to explore the extent to which you use closed forms of words in difficult conversations at work.

The closed-to-learning model: closed forms of words

In Chapter 3, we described the first part of the closed-to-learning model – the three characteristics of closed-to-learning *thinking*. In this chapter we consider the second part of this model – those components of closed conversation that are identifiable in the *forms of words* we find ourselves using as a result of closed-to-learning thinking. We do this so that we will be able to identify the forms of words that we find ourselves using and to see how these contribute to the ineffectiveness or effectiveness of the way that we manage our own difficult conversations.

We defined the term 'forms of words' in Chapter 2 as the ways in which we express our closed or open-to-learning thinking during a conversation. If our thinking is closed-to-learning, the forms of words that we use – and that the other person hears – will reflect that way of thinking. This means that they will reflect the three characteristics of closed-to-learning thinking we outlined in the previous chapter.

When we fail to question our assumptions (Characteristic One), our forms of words convey our taken-for-granted belief that our way of seeing things is the right way and that there is little room for negotiation. They work against making the conversation a partnership (Characteristic Two), and they also lack the informational content that is required for an informed discussion of difficulties (Characteristic Three). In these ways they both express our closed-to-learning ways of thinking and, because they cut us off from feedback and learning that could change the way we think, they also reinforce it. The result is a conversation in which difficulties are not discussed, or not discussed effectively.

The effects of closed-to-learning thinking on advocacy and inquiry

We introduced the terms 'advocacy' and 'inquiry' in Chapter 2 to describe two forms of words that are common to all conversations. 'Advocacy' refers to those statements we make that convey information about the way we see things. As such it describes the way we give expression to our wishes, views, feelings or concerns. Advocacy may also communicate background reasoning and information that is relevant to our viewpoint or position. 'Inquiry' refers to questions we ask that seek to elicit information from the other person about their wishes, views, feelings or problems. Inquiry may also include requests for more general information or the reasoning relevant to the other person's viewpoint or situation.

If our thinking is closed-to-learning, we automatically produce types of advocacy and inquiry that are closed-to-learning – closed advocacy and closed inquiry. These closed forms of words perpetuate the ineffective handling of difficult conversations and lead to adverse outcomes.

In this chapter we look at each of these closed forms of words in turn, their relationship with closed-to-learning thinking and the impact they have on difficult conversations.

Closed advocacy

Closed-to-learning thinking results in advocacy that is closed. Advocacy can be closed in two ways: first, when 'advocacy is not transparent' and, second, when we do not link our advocacy with an inquiry – we call this 'advocacy without inquiry'.

Advocacy is not transparent

Advocacy that comes from closed-to-learning thinking lacks transparency. By this we mean that we express views and make comments that do not include the sort of information that enables the listener to assess the validity of what we say and thus make an informed response. This limits the scope of the feedback that we receive and so contributes to keeping us trapped in closed-to-learning mode. Lack of transparency also means giving advocacy that misleads, in that it reflects strategic, closed-to-learning thinking. What follows describes some of the ways in which our advocacy often lacks transparency.

We state our views without including enough background information

> *Examples*
> 'It's not a job for a woman.'
> 'The management structure needs re-organising.'

Assertive statements such as these, made without further explanation, reflect Characteristic Three of closed-to-learning thinking (We do not promote the exchange of all relevant information.) Each of the examples above is a bare assertion of the speaker's personal interpretation, theory or conclusion. The statements do not include any context, data or reasoning that might allow the other person to understand the thinking behind the views being expressed and so be in a position to assess their worth.

Such uninformative statements leave the listener at a disadvantage. Not only are listeners unable to assess the validity of the speaker's statement, they are also not in a position to challenge the data or reasoning on which those statements are based. Consequently, they are unable to make an informed response.

For instance, in the second of the above examples ('The management structure needs re-organising'), the listener may be left uncertain as to whether this is just the speaker's opinion, or whether there is documented evidence to back it up – a consultant's report, for example. Because of this uncertainty, the listener is in no position to respond with informed comments that could contribute to a useful discussion.

If a listener is obliged to respond in ignorance of the background information or reasoning relating to remarks made, there is also a risk that they will base their response on a misunderstanding. For instance, in the case of the above example 'It's not a job for a woman', a female listener might conclude that such a remark was intended as a put-down when this might not have been the intention, and respond defensively or with anger.

We also disadvantage the listener when our statements express an opinion about them, or about a third party, without any explanation as to what it was that led us to come to our conclusion, as in the following examples.

Examples
'You handled that situation badly.'
'That was a good presentation.'
'She has no idea how to dress for the office.'

Thus, in the first example above, the listener hears the speaker's negative opinion, but not what it was about their handling of the situation that gave rise to that opinion. The difficulty that might need to be discussed is not identified. When we make a criticism without supporting evidence we risk evoking an ill-informed, defensive or confrontational response from the other person. This is likely to produce a defensive response in us, making it virtually impossible for concerns to be discussed as partners.

The listener may be equally disadvantaged when the judgement is intended as a compliment. For example, the statement 'That was a good presentation', does not tell the listener what it was about the presentation that was good. As a result, they may be left wondering whether the speaker really meant what they said, or whether they were just being polite. In neither of these examples, does the listener get information of a kind that would enable them to resolve any possible misunderstandings.

Sometimes we provide evidence for our judgements and evaluations yet do this by appealing to common knowledge or received wisdom. This is the case with phrases like 'As we all know...' (for example, '... Mr S is unreliable'), or 'It's a well-established fact that...' (for example, '... men make better drivers'). However, appealing to 'knowledge' that is both vague or difficult to verify, rather than giving information that makes clear the validity of our statement, still disadvantages the listener and makes it unlikely that they will be able to respond to what we are saying in a useful way.

We give information that sidesteps the issue and/or is misleading

Sometimes our advocacy lacks transparency in the sense that, as part of a strategic approach to a difficulty, we give non-relevant or misleading information that may sidestep the issue or conceal the true picture.

Example

A manager who is afraid give a practitioner the real answer (that he has poor interpersonal skills) to his question about why he has not been promoted, says: 'We rate you very highly – we value what you do; the contracts you've secured, the work you do – you're a very valued employee.'

[This example is taken from Conversation 1 on page 79]

Although the manager appears to back up her statement 'We rate you very highly' with further detail ('the contracts you've secured, the work you do'), her whole speech is designed to avoid having to give a straight answer to the practitioner's question.

Advocacy without inquiry

The problems created by advocacy that lacks adequate supporting information are compounded if no inquiry is used to seek a response from the other person. This again serves to limit feedback that might cause us to question our assumptions and so contributes to keeping us trapped in closed-to-learning mode.

Advocacy without inquiry arises from Characteristic Two (We do not promote partnership) and Characteristic Three (We do not promote the exchange of all relevant information) and carries them into our conversation.

The following are examples of the ways in which we give advocacy without inquiry:

We make statements without checking the other person's response

Our own data from practitioners' scripts of their difficult conversations shows that advocacy without inquiry is the most common form of words to appear in difficult conversations that are ineffectively managed. When our thinking is closed-to-learning, we focus mainly on putting forward our own position. An informed onlooker is likely to be able to identify a good deal of advocacy – statements of where we stand – in what we say. At the same time, they will notice an absence of appropriate and timely checking out of the other person's response.

Examples

'I've explained what has been going on,' (without 'Did my explanation make sense to you?')

'I'm confident the re-organisation plans will work very well,' (without

'Do you agree?')

'I want to start our discussion by telling you what was said on the course I went to,' (without 'Are you happy for us to start here?')

'Here are my holiday snaps,' (without, 'Would you like to see them?')

When we advocate our position without checking out the other person's response to what we have said, we risk communicating the message that we are not interested in hearing their viewpoint. This can leave the listener feeling disadvantaged, risk producing bad feeling and a defensive reaction, and can lead to a conversation that is difficult to handle. It can also face the listener with the difficulty of expressing an alternative point of view without this coming over as confrontational: for example in response to 'I'm confident the re-organisation plans will work very well', where the other person is not asked whether or not they agree.

We speak at length without inviting a response from the other person

In an effort to express our views, we sometimes find ourselves speaking at length. In the process, we can make a considerable number of statements without inviting a response from the other person. This can create problems. For example, the listener experiences an information overload and switches off, or the conversation becomes unfocused because the listener does not know which point to respond to. Furthermore, the listener is given the chance to pick and choose which of our statements to respond to.

Closed inquiry

Inquiry can be closed-to-learning in two main ways. First, when a question does not constitute a genuine request for information we say that 'inquiry is not genuine'. Second, when we ask a question without saying why we are asking, we call this 'inquiry without advocacy'.

Inquiry is not genuine

Inquiry may not be genuine in a number of ways:

Our request for a response to what we say comes over as lacking any real desire to hear the other person's viewpoint

Example

'So we're all agreed on this strategy. Yes?' (indicating a lack of interest in the reply by putting papers away)

In this example the verbal request for others' views is contradicted by the non-verbal aspects of the speaker's behaviour – putting papers away. This risks communicating a lack of interest in the others' response and hence undermining listeners' confidence in the genuineness of the verbal inquiry.

We ask (rhetorical) questions that lack genuine information-seeking intent

Some questions give a semblance of inquiry, but in reality the speaker is expressing their own opinion and expecting the listener to go along with what they say. They do not genuinely seek the listener's opinion. If we have no intention of allowing the other person's response to alter what we think, such 'inquiry' will simply perpetuate what is already a closed position.

> *Examples*
> 'Surely you don't mean that?'
> 'Haven't you got anything better to do?'
> 'That's not appropriate dress for staff is it?'
> 'Why don't you think it over?' (while turning away)

Rhetorical questions can have a negative effect on difficult conversations. In conveying an assumption that the other person will agree with what we say, such questions exert pressure on the other person not to contradict us. The other person may feel that they are being manoeuvred into going along with a view with which they do not agree. They may then respond defensively or not at all. Thus difficulties are made undiscussable and hard to deal with.

Some rhetorical questions may also come over as put-downs, as with, 'Haven't you got anything better to do?' These may be perceived as (veiled) attacks and are likely to provoke a negative reaction.

Inquiry without advocacy

Inquiry without advocacy refers to the following:

We ask questions without giving our reasons for asking them

When our thinking is closed-to-learning, it can lead us to ask questions (inquiry...) without giving our reasons for asking them (... without advocacy).

Examples

'What are you doing Tuesday lunchtime?'

'How do you think it went?' (before giving feedback on a colleague's presentation)

'Are you the homeowner?' (telephone call)

'Where have you been?'

Inquiry without advocacy can prevent a useful exchange of information and add to the difficulty of a conversation. Because we do not tell the listener why we are we are asking the question, they may give a response based on guessing our motives. They are not in a position to give an informed and considered reply. While this disadvantages the listener, it can also disadvantage us, in that we may not receive the information we need. For example, we may wish to know the answer to our question, 'What are you doing Tuesday lunchtime?' in order to find out if the other person would be available for a lunchtime outing. However, if we do not say why we are asking the question, the other person may guess that being seen to be available could be to their disadvantage and try to avoid giving us the information we want.

Inquiry without advocacy may result from our unawareness of what the other person needs to know – a feature of Characteristic Three of closed-to-learning thinking (We do not promote the exchange of all relevant information). However, inquiry without advocacy can also result from the tactical pursuit of our own agenda – a feature of Characteristic Two (We do not promote partnership). For example, the thinking behind questions such as 'How did you think it went?' might be: 'If I find out his reaction first it will give me some clue as to how to pitch my criticism', or, 'I hope she already realises that her presentation was poor so that I won't have to be the one to say so'. Whatever the reasons for the inquiry, they are not disclosed.

Exercises for identifying closed advocacy and closed inquiry and their effects on a conversation

Advocacy is not transparent

- In the course of your working day, listen for any occasions when those engaged in the conversation make statements about individuals using words like 'good', 'useless', 'conscientious', 'lazy' (*advocacy...*), without supporting evidence (*...is not transparent*), or when they express views or feelings without giving their reasons for these. Note whether this lack of explanatory information has any effects on the conversation.

- Try to become aware of times when you yourself fail to give adequate background information when making a statement and whether, as a result, the conversation becomes difficult to handle.

- Notice when you are tempted to give information that sidesteps the issue or that may conceal the truth of a situation.

- Notice when you give information with an air of certainty, when the basis for that information is, in fact, a personal opinion or a spurious claim.

Advocacy without inquiry

- Identify a conversation in which two people are putting forward conflicting views (*advocacy...*). Look for any moments in the conversation when one of them might have made some timely inquiry about the other person's position, such as 'Do you agree?' or 'Do you understand my position?' but failed to do so (*... without inquiry*).

- Notice when a person to whom you are talking gives you their views (*advocacy...*) but does not ask you whether or not you understand or agree with them (*...without inquiry*). Identify any difficulty you may have in expressing a lack of understanding or disagreement with their views when they are presented in this way.

- Try to become aware of times when someone responds in a negative manner when you make a statement (*advocacy...*) without checking out the other person's response (*...without inquiry*).

Inquiry is not genuine

- Observe how you feel when people ask you a question *(inquiry...)* in a way that makes it quite clear that they expect your agreement *(...is not genuine)*, but when you actually disagree.

- Try to catch any instances when you yourself use a rhetorical question as a means of eliciting agreement.

Inquiry without advocacy

- In the course of your working day, notice when someone asks another person a question *(inquiry...)* without saying why he or she is asking it *(...without advocacy)*.

- Identify times when the person you are talking to asks you a question *(inquiry...)* but leaves you uncertain as to why they are asking it *(...without advocacy)*. Does this shape your reply in a negative way? If so, why?

- Become aware of times when you ask a question *(inquiry...)* in circumstances when you prefer not to disclose why you are asking it *(...without advocacy)*.

Key exercise step 3:

Evaluating your words in terms of the closed-to-learning model

Instructions for Step 3 of the Key Exercise are to be found in Appendix B under the heading **'Evaluating your words in terms of the closed-to-learning model'** (page 246). This will guide you to evaluate your words, in the difficult conversation you recorded in Step 1, in terms of the closed forms of advocacy and inquiry described in this chapter.

5

Annotated Examples of the Closed-to-Learning Approach

Learning points

How the closed-to-learning approach plays out in ten difficult conversations.

How the closed-to-learning approach results in adverse outcomes for each of the ten conversations.

In Chapter 1 we identified ten types of difficult conversation at work. In this chapter we look at some annotated examples of closed-to-learning, ineffective approaches to these ten types of difficult conversation, listed below.

The ten types of difficult conversation

1. Saying something critical.
2. Communicating unwelcome information that we are obliged to convey.
3. Saying something we think will go against group consensus.
4. Retrieving a setback in an interpersonal relationship.
5. Engaging with someone who will not discuss things with us.
6. Dealing with a conflict of loyalties.
7. Coping with being criticised.
8. Responding to non-verbal behaviour that bothers us.
9. Responding to pressure to go beyond what we feel comfortable with.
10. Handling a conflict of views between ourselves and another person.

The examples are based on conversations that practitioners have brought to our courses and workshops. Although the difficult conversations at work in which readers are involved may be different in their detail from these examples, it is likely that readers' own difficult conversations will have much in common with one or more of the ten *types* of difficulty presented here. Our annotations are intended to offer the kind of analysis that can be applied to *all* difficult conversations.[7]

How the annotated examples are set out

The difficult conversations in this chapter involve two people. We call them *A* and *B*. *A* is the person whose handling of the conversation we focus on and to whose thoughts we have access. Each example begins with a description of the difficulty that *A* faces in relation to the conversation concerned.

The conversations are laid out in two columns. The right-hand column shows the words spoken by *A* and *B*, the left-hand column shows *A*'s thoughts. *A*'s thoughts and words are numbered consecutively.

The analysis that follows the conversation relates *A*'s thoughts and words to the components (characteristics and closed forms of words) of the closed conversation model described in Chapters 3 and 4. To assist that analysis, *A*'s thoughts and words are repeated in the annotations, making use of the numbering already given.

As a reminder, we set out again the characteristics and forms of words typical of the closed conversation model:

Thoughts:

Characteristic One:	We do not question our assumptions.
Characteristic Two:	We do not promote partnership.
Characteristic Three:	We do not promote the exchange of all relevant information.

Forms of words:

Closed advocacy:
- Advocacy is not transparent.
- Advocacy without inquiry.

Closed inquiry:
- Inquiry is not genuine.
- Inquiry without advocacy.

---

[7] For the annotated *open* version of these conversations, see Chapter 9.

Why we focus on person A

We focus our attention on person *A* for a number of reasons. First, we take *A* to represent us – the person who is trying to manage a difficult conversation. We are concerned primarily with *A* (representing us) because it is only our own contribution over which we have any direct control. However much (as *A*) we may wish the other person (*B*) to act differently, we do not have the power to make them do so. While it is our experience that an improvement in *A*'s skills will often bring about positive changes in *B*'s response, and thereby assist in resolving the difficulties faced, ultimately it is only through our (*A*'s) understanding and skills that there is any reliable way of effectively addressing the tough issues underlying our difficult conversations.

We also focus on *A* because we only know the thinking that is going on behind the words that *A* speaks. Although we may sometimes *assume* we know what others (*B*) are thinking, in reality we only have reliable access to our own thoughts, not to those of others and we can therefore only change our own thinking directly.

For the above reasons, we feel that insight and understanding are best gained by putting ourselves in *A*'s position in reading through these examples.

1. Saying something critical (closed approach)

A, a manager, is finding it difficult to tell *B* that the reason he (*B*) has not been promoted is because of his poor interpersonal skills.

How might *A* deal with her difficulty?

A's thoughts	A and B's words
	B. I notice that over the last couple of years many of the people who've got the same sort of qualifications and experience as me are getting promotion or getting more responsibility. I'm not... and I'm wondering why that is...is there something the company's trying to tell me?

(1) Oh dear, I was afraid this might come up. The real reason I haven't recommended him for promotion is that I've got concerns about his interpersonal skills...

...but I'm worried about saying that...there's no way he could cope with me telling him the real problem...

so I'll suggest that it's nothing personal and reassure him that we really value him.

A. (1) Oh, I don't think so – it's just one of those things... we rate you very highly – we value what you do; the contracts you've secured, the work you do – you're a very valued employee.

B. Yes – but that's what you said last time round. I suppose what I really want to ask you is 'OK then, when am I going to get my promotion or additional responsibilities?'

(2) He's trying to pin me down... but I really can't tell him what the problem is... I'll give a vague explanation... and reassure him again.

A. (2) Well these things aren't quite so straight forward – there are so many factors at work in deciding when people are moved up the scale... such as whether there's a vacancy, the state of the company finances... I really don't think you've got anything to worry about.

B. Maybe, but I still don't understand why it's only me that hasn't been promoted.

Oh, dear, I don't think he's been as reassured as I intended.

.

A's thoughts and words, evaluated in terms of the components of the closed conversation model

Thoughts (1)

'Oh dear, I was afraid this might come up. The real reason I haven't recommended him for promotion is that I've got concerns about his interpersonal skills... but I'm worried about saying that... there's no way he could cope with me telling him the real problem...so I'll suggest that it's nothing personal and reassure him that we really value him.'

Characteristic One (We do not question our assumptions). We can see from *A*'s thoughts that, even before the conversation begins, she makes an assumption ('there's no way he could cope with me telling her the real problem'). *A* feels no need to question this assumption. So she is limited to approaching *B*'s question in a way that avoids telling him that she has concerns about his interpersonal skills ('so I'll suggest that it's nothing personal and that we really value him').

Characteristic Two (We do not promote partnership). Because of her unquestioned assumption, *A* sees no need to involve *B* in the way she manages the conversation. Thus, without reference to *B*'s thoughts or feelings, she unilaterally tries to protect *B* (from what she believes he cannot cope with) by moving the conversation away from the central issue and onto safer ground. Nor does she involve *B* as a partner in negotiating the focus of the conversation by trying to find out what *B* would find helpful.

Characteristic Three (We do not promote the exchange of all relevant information). Again, because of her unquestioned assumption, *A* fails to give *B* the one piece of relevant information he needs in order to understand the real reason why he has not been given promotion. Rather than looking for ways of telling him about these concerns, *A* beats about the bush in order to avoid this crucial issue.

Words (1)

'Oh, I don't think so – it's just one of those things... we rate you very highly – we value what you do; the contracts you've secured, the work you do – you're a very valued employee.'

Closed advocacy (Advocacy is not transparent). *A* makes irrelevant comments that avoid answering *B*'s question ('... we rate you very highly

... we value what you do... you're a very valued employee') and therefore do not give him the information he needs. **B** may not know what to make of these statements, or may see them as empty reassurance.

Closed advocacy (Advocacy without inquiry). Because **A** simply makes comments and does not ask for any response from **B**, her words do not lead to any kind of joint engagement with **B**'s concerns.

Thoughts (2)

'He's trying to pin me down... but I really can't tell him what the problem is... I'll give a vague explanation... and reassure him again.'

Characteristic One (We do not question our assumptions). Because **A**'s assumption has trapped her into responding in a certain way, she has no choice but to continue to think in the same way ('... I really can't tell him what the problem is... I'll give a vague explanation... and reassure him again').

Characteristic Three (We do not promote the exchange of all relevant information). By deliberately planning to leave her explanations vague ('I'll give him a vague explanation') **A** gives **B** little basis either for questioning the explanations, or for assessing how valid they are.

Words (2)

'Well these things aren't quite so straight forward – there are so many factors at work in deciding when people are moved up the scale... such as whether there's a vacancy, the state of the company finances... I really don't think you've got anything to worry about.'

Closed advocacy (Advocacy is not transparent). **A** again gives irrelevant reassurance ('I don't think you've got anything to worry about'), that conceals the real reason why **B** has not been promoted.

Closed advocacy (Advocacy without inquiry). **A** makes no attempt to inquire about **B**'s response to what she has said.

Summary

A's unquestioned assumption that **B** would not cope with the real reason for his lack of promotion prevents her from communicating this information. The sensitive, but crucial, issue of **B**'s poor interpersonal skills is thus not made discussable.

Outcomes

Although *A* has got through a difficult conversation without having to deal with *B*'s reaction to the real reason for his lack of promotion, she has done so only at the cost of a number of adverse outcomes.

For A. A has not succeeded in overcoming her difficulty with telling *B* the real reason for his lack of promotion. She may therefore well be left feeling uncomfortable and lacking in competence.

For A and B's relationship. There will be discomfort for both because of an unaddressed and unresolved issue, and a potentially recurring scenario each time *B* fails to get promotion (with a possibly increasingly embittered *B*).

For the organisation. Because *B* still does not know the reason for his lack of promotion he is unlikely to do anything about improving his interpersonal skills. The organisation will have to continue to accommodate his weaknesses.

[For the annotated *open* version of Conversation 1, see Chapter 9, page 157.]

2. Communicating unwelcome information that we are obliged to convey (closed approach)

A, a manager, has to tell *B*, a member of staff, that she is to be re-located. *A* is finding this difficult because he fears that *B* may be upset by the decision.

How might *A* deal with his difficulty?

A's thoughts	*A* and *B*'s words
(1) I'm not looking forward to this. *B*'s going to be furious about the relocation decision – it'll mean further travelling for her and it may upset her childcare arrangements. But the decision's been made. So I need to try and soften the blow…present the move in a positive light and let her know we're there for her.	

	A. (1) **B**, I asked to see you because I have to inform you that from the first of next month you will be working from our office on the south side of the city. You'll find the surroundings very pleasant and I'm sure you'll be very happy there – it's actually quite a privilege to be chosen for the move. Anyway do think about it and please don't hesitate to let us know if there's anything we can do.
	B. I don't believe this. Why haven't I been consulted? And why me? Have you any idea how this move might affect my domestic arrangements! Why can't you transfer someone without children?
(2) Oh dear. Just as I thought. I knew she'd be angry. What should I do now?… I'll be sympathetic and reassuring but firm…	
	A. (2) I'm sorry you're upset… but I'm afraid the decision has been made…why don't you think it over?… you're a very adaptable person… I'm sure things will work out fine…
	B. I'm sure they'll work out fine for you! I now have to 'think about' how I'm going to rearrange my life. (**B** walks out)

A's thoughts and words, evaluated in terms of the components of the closed conversation model

Thoughts (1)

'I'm not looking forward to this. **B**'s going to be furious about the re-location decision – it'll mean further travelling for her and it may upset her child-care arrangements. But the decision's been made. So I need to try and soften the blow… present the move in a positive light and let her know we're there for her.'

Characteristic One (We do not question our assumptions). **A** makes two unquestioned assumptions. First that '**B**'s going to be furious about the relocation decision'. Because **A** does not question this assumption, it leads to a second unquestioned assumption about the best way to handle such a situation ('I need to soften the blow'). Because neither of these assumptions is questioned, they are allowed to determine the closed-to-learning nature of **A**'s contribution to the conversation.

Characteristic Two (We do not promote partnership). Because from the outset **A** is dominated by his own view of the situation, he does not involve **B** in the way that the conversation is managed. Thus, in planning to pursue his own agenda without asking for a response from **B**, **A** tries to avoid having to deal with **B**'s actual thoughts and feelings.

Characteristic Three (We do not promote the exchange of all relevant information). **A** knows that he must deliver his news. But what he plans to offer is information that is relevant to his own, undisclosed strategy of presenting the move in a positive light. This is not necessarily relevant to **B**'s concerns (for example, '... let her know we're there for her'). Furthermore, **A** does not offer **B** information that is relevant to her – who made the relocation decision and the reasoning behind it.

Words (1)

'... I asked to see you because I have to inform you that from the first of next month you will be working from our office on the south side of the city. You'll find the surroundings very pleasant and I'm sure you'll be very happy there – it's actually quite a privilege to be chosen for the move. Anyway do think about it and please don't hesitate to let us know if there's anything we can do.'

Closed advocacy (Advocacy is not transparent). **A** opens the conversation in a way that literally reflects his unquestioned assumptions. He states the facts (because he is obliged to do so) but then tries to soften the blow by trying to put the relocation decision in a good light. However, his comments ('You'll find the surroundings very pleasant and I'm sure you'll be happy there – it's actually quite a privilege to be chosen for the move') lack transparency because he is not able to let **B** know why he is saying this without disclosing his strategy.

Closed advocacy (Advocacy without inquiry). **A** does not use inquiry to find out **B**'s response to what he has said, nor to ask **B** how she would like the conversation to proceed. *B* may feel that *A* is controlling the conversation in a way that prevents him from having to deal with any negative reaction she, *B*, may have.

Thoughts (2)

> 'Oh dear. Just as I thought. I knew she'd be angry. What should I do now? I'll be sympathetic and reassuring but firm...'

Characteristic One (We do not question our assumptions). When *B* responds angrily, *A*, believing his first unquestioned assumption to be confirmed ('Just as I thought...'), can think of nothing else but repeat his attempts to make the decision acceptable to *B* ('I'll be sympathetic and reassuring...').

Words (2)

> 'I'm sorry you're upset... but I'm afraid the decision has been made...why don't you think it over?... you're a very adaptable person...I'm sure things will work out fine...'

Closed advocacy (Advocacy is not transparent). Although *A* briefly acknowledges *B*'s feelings, he then downplays them ('I'm sorry you're upset...but...you're a very adaptable person... I'm sure things will work out fine'). As a result, *B* is likely to perceive *A*'s expression of concern ('I'm sorry you're upset') as superficial and insincere. Nor does *A* give reasons for his flattering comments ('It's quite a privilege to be chosen', or, 'you're a very adaptable person'), thus increasing the chances that *B* will perceive these words as insincere.

Closed inquiry (Inquiry is not genuine). *A*'s one question ('... why don't you think it over?') is rhetorical in nature and is likely to be perceived by *B* as an empty phrase rather than a genuine inquiry that invites a choice of response.

Summary

Although *A* achieves his managerial task of letting *B* know that she is to be re-located, his unquestioned assumption that he can predict *B*'s reaction prevents him from doing so in a way that acknowledges that the relocation decision may create a problem for *B*. *B*'s concerns are deflected and not made discussable in a way that she finds acceptable, and *B* makes her reaction to the conversation clear by walking out on *A*.

Outcomes

A feels relieved that he has succeeded in his duty of telling *B* that she is to be relocated and that she has got it over quickly. But his (*A*'s) approach has nevertheless resulted in a number of adverse outcomes.

For A. A may well feel hurt at being attacked as the messenger when he was clearly trying to make the unpleasant information as easy as possible for *B* to accept. He may also feel a lack of competence because, although he managed to tell *B* what he needed to tell her, the conversation ended with *B* walking out on him.

For A and B's relationship. Given *B*'s anger – not only at the news but possibly also at *A*'s attempts to play down her difficulties – this episode does not bode well for any possible working relationship between *A* and *B* in the future.

For the organisation. The organisation now has a member of staff, *B*, whose commitment and confidence in the management may be adversely affected by the way the news of her relocation was handled.

[For the annotated *open* version of Conversation 2, see Chapter 9, page 161.]

3. Saying something we think will go against group consensus (closed approach)

A, a section manager, is attending one of his monthly meetings with a group of other section managers, *B* being the chairperson. *A* increasingly feels that the meetings take up a lot of his time and that they are not particularly productive. However, he is worried that if he brings this up he may provoke hostility from in his colleagues.

How might *A* deal with his difficulty?

A's thoughts	A and B's words
I'm so fed up with these meetings – they take up the whole afternoon…	*B.* Has anyone got any issues they'd like to raise under AOB?

whether there's anything important to discuss or not... nothing particularly useful comes out of them for me... (1) I'd really like to tell the others, but I'm worried that if I say anything negative about the meetings... which they seem to enjoy... I'm bound to get their backs up... and then they'll close ranks on me and make me feel even worse. ...it's probably better just to grin and bear it..	*A*. (1) (remains silent) *B*. ...No? Alright. I'll book the room for the same time next month – see you all then.

A's thoughts and words, evaluated in terms of the components of the closed conversation model

Thoughts (1)

'I'd really like to tell the others, but I'm worried that if I say anything negative about the meetings... which they seem to enjoy... I'm bound to get their backs up... and then they'll close ranks on me and make me feel even worse... it's probably better just to grin and bear it...'

Characteristic One (We do not question our assumptions). A makes a number of assumptions about his colleagues' likely reaction if he expresses his dissatisfaction with the meetings ('I'm bound to get their backs up... they'll close ranks on me and make me feel even worse'). Since A does not question these, they drive him into silence about his worries, at the cost of having to put up with the current situation.

Characteristic Two (We do not promote partnership). To avoid risking his colleagues' negative reactions, A makes a private decision not to initiate discussion about the issue.

Characteristic Three (We do not promote the exchange of all relevant information). Because he is constrained by his worry about his colleagues' likely response, *A* decides not to disclose what is for him an important problem.

Words (1)

(remains silent)

Absence of both advocacy and inquiry. In saying nothing *A* avoids both disclosing his own problem with the meetings and finding out his colleagues' position.

Summary

A's unquestioned assumption that his colleagues will close ranks against him if he communicates his concerns about the meetings prevents him from even raising his difficulty. There is therefore no chance of his concerns being discussed.

Outcomes

Although *A* has avoided the risk of provoking hostility from his colleagues, he has done so at the cost of the following adverse outcomes.

For A. A is left stuck with a pattern of meetings that shows no signs of changing. He may also feel annoyed with himself for not taking the opportunity to raise the issue.

For A and B's relationship. A's frustration at having to attend the meetings may well show in the way he interacts with his colleagues in future meetings.

For the organisation. An organisational issue – the possibility that time is being wasted – does not get aired.

[For the annotated *open* version of Conversation 3, see Chapter 9, page 166.]

4. Retrieving a setback in an interpersonal relationship (closed approach)

A, a manager knows that *B*, a member of her staff, is angry with her, because she was abrupt with *B* in a recent conversation. *A* wants to restore a positive working relationship with *B* but she is anxious that in doing this she will lose credibility as a manager.

How might *A* deal with her difficulty?

A's thoughts	*A* and *B*'s words
(1) I know that *B*'s angry with me because I snapped at her this morning... I shouldn't have done that...but on the other hand *B* should have known better than to choose a moment when I'm busy to give me her views. I'd like to put things right but I'm feeling quite uncomfortable because it doesn't look good for a manager to apologise or admit blame... Best thing to do is to act as though it never happened.	
	A. (1) *B*, can we talk about the conference schedule for next week? *B*. Well I'll listen to what you have to say but I'm not sure I want to have a discussion if I'm going to get my head bitten off again.
(2) Oh dear. She really is angry...never mind... stay calm... and just remind her that I value her views. That way she's likely to see that it wasn't anything serious and we can get back to where we were.	
	A. (2) Oh, come on *B*...you know I value your opinion and...

	B. That's not what it seemed like this morning.
This doesn't seem to be working...	

A's thoughts and words, evaluated in terms of the components of the closed conversation model

Thoughts (1)

'I know that **B**'s angry with me because I snapped at her this morning... I shouldn't have done that... but on the other hand **B** should have known better than to choose a moment when I'm busy to give me her views. I'd like to put things right but I'm feeling quite uncomfortable because it doesn't look good for a manager to apologise or admit blame... Best thing to do is to act as though it never happened.'

Characteristic One (We do not question our assumptions). A assumes that although she has done something she now regrets (snapped at *B*) it would not be appropriate for her as a manager to apologise or admit blame. Because she does not question this assumption, she is compelled to override her own feeling that there is a need to put things right. Thus she is forced into strategies designed to downplay what has happened by suggesting that nothing untoward has occurred.

Characteristic Three (We do not promote the exchange of all relevant information). A keeps to herself a number of her own thoughts and feelings which are very relevant to dealing with her problem. However, in the light of her unquestioned assumptions about her role as manager, she feels too embarrassed or nervous to reveal these thoughts ('I snapped at her this morning... I shouldn't have done that... I'd like to put things right but I'm feeling quite uncomfortable...').

Words (1)

'**B**, can we talk about the conference schedule for next week?'

Closed inquiry (Inquiry without advocacy). A asks *B* a question ('**B**, can we talk about the conference schedule for next week?') without giving her real reason for asking it, which is to steer *B* away from what had happened in the morning. In the light of the earlier setback in their relationship, *A*'s

91

entirely work-related question – which makes no reference to her earlier behaviour towards **B** – may well come over to **B** as demonstrating an uncaring attitude.

Thoughts (2)

> 'Oh dear. She really is angry... never mind... stay calm... and just remind her that I value her views. That way she's likely to see that it wasn't anything serious so we can get back to where we were.'

Characteristic Two (We do not promote partnership). **A** overrides her feeling that she needs to get involved with **B** in discussing what had happened in the morning. Her private agenda is to protect herself by trying to ignore feelings on both sides and 'act as though it never happened'. Therefore when **B** makes it clear that she is still angry, **A** attempts to maintain her stance by staying calm, suggesting to **B** that 'it wasn't anything serious' and placating her ('remind her that I value her views').

Words (2)

> 'Oh, come on **B**... you know I value your opinion and...'

Closed advocacy (Advocacy is not transparent). **A**'s words are presented without any supporting evidence that might convince **B** that, after the morning's events, **A** really does value her views. In the absence of any such evidence these statements are likely to come over as a put-down ('Oh, come on **B**'), as an insincere attempt at appeasement ('you know I value your opinion'), or both.

Summary

A's strategy of trying to ignore what had happened in the morning, forced on her by her assumptions about what is and is not appropriate for a manager to do, prevents the difficulty – the setback in the relationship – from becoming discussable.

Outcomes

A may or may not have succeeded in retaining her credibility as a manager. Even if she has, it is at the cost of a number of adverse outcomes.

For A. **A** has not succeeded in restoring a positive working relationship with **B**. She may well feel that, as a manager, she handled the conversation badly.

For A and B's relationship. The tensions of the morning remain unresolved and do not offer a good basis for *A* and *B*'s future working relationship.

For the organisation. The organisation has to live with the continuing tension between a manager and one of her staff.

[For the annotated *open* version of Conversation 4, see Chapter 9, page 169.]

5. Engaging with someone who will not discuss things with us (closed approach)

A, a hard pressed administrative assistant, is, once again, given even more work that is urgent by her senior manager. On past experience *A* believes it will be pointless to say 'no', as *B* does not take her problem seriously.

How might *A* deal with her difficulty?

A's thoughts	*A* and *B*'s words
	B. A, I need the Departmental Progress Report completed urgently – the meeting's been brought forward to tomorrow.
(1) Oh no!... I'm already up to here with his urgent work... I'll tell him that it's impossible... but I'm feeling really stressed because he never listens to me.	
	A. (1) Look, I really can't take any more on – I'm fully stretched as it is...
	B. I know. We're all under pressure aren't we... but this really is urgent... and I'm sure I can rely on you to find a way of fitting it in.
(2) I knew he wouldn't listen to me.	

A's thoughts and words, evaluated in terms of the components of the closed conversation model

Thoughts (1)

'Oh no!... I'm already up to here with his urgent work... I'll tell him that it's impossible... but I'm feeling really stressed because he never listens to me.'

Characteristic One (We do not question our assumptions). **A** goes into this conversation with an unquestioned assumption that there can be no discussion or resolution of the problem because **B** 'never listens to her'.

Words (1)

'Look, I really can't take any more on – I'm fully stretched as it is...'

Closed advocacy (Advocacy without inquiry). **A** makes her problem of being overstretched clear to **B** ('I really can't take any more on – I'm fully stretched with urgent work as it is...'). However, **A** does not use any inquiry. She neither asks **B** whether he understands her position nor invites **B** into a discussion of the problem. Because of **A**'s lack of inquiry, **B** is able to follow his own agenda and make sympathetic and flattering noises that avoid engagement with **A**'s problem.

Thoughts (2)

'I knew he wouldn't listen to me.'

Characteristic One (We do not question our assumptions). When **B** duly responds to **A**'s protests in an offhand way, **A** takes his words as a confirmation of her assumption that she will not be able to get **B** to take her problem seriously.

Characteristic Two (We do not promote partnership). Because of her certainty **A** sees no point in making any further attempt to discuss the situation.

Summary

Although some important difficulties are made explicit in this conversation – the urgency of **B**'s work, **A**'s sense of overload – **A** is unable to take the next step in making the difficulties discussable and engage **B** as a partner in the conversation.

Outcomes

Although **A** may feel relieved to have avoided any immediate conflict with her manager, her continued strategy of giving in to his demands has resulted in adverse outcomes.

For A. **A** has not succeeded in getting **B** to take her problem seriously. She is now faced with the task of fitting in **B**'s work somehow. She is likely to be left feeling undervalued and resentful as well as stressed by her increased, urgent workload.

For A and B's relationship. **A**'s resentment with the way that **B** exploits the imbalance in power is likely to be reinforced as a result of this conversation.

For the organisation. The organisation is likely to end up with a burnt-out administrative assistant, or with the Departmental Progress Report (and probably some of **B**'s other tasks) completed by the deadline but, very likely, to a lower standard than might otherwise have been the case.

[For the annotated *open* version of Conversation 5, see Chapter 9, page 173.]

6. Dealing with a conflict of loyalties (closed approach)

A, a manager, is approached by a member of staff, **B**, with a complaint that **B**'s colleague **X**, is not pulling her weight and that **B** wishes to work with someone else. **A** is sympathetic to **B**'s situation but has been told, in confidence, that **X** is on medication that affects her concentration and should be protected from any changes that might add to her problems. **A** feels a conflict of loyalties between his sympathy for **B** and his wish to protect **X**.

How might **A** deal with his difficulty?

A's thoughts	**A** and **B**'s words
	B. A, I'm not at all happy to go on working with **X**. She's not been pulling her weight recently and I constantly have to cover for her. Do you think you could arrange for me to work with someone else?

(1) I'm torn between the two of them! I can see **B**'s problem but **X** needs stability... and I can't tell **B** about **X**'s difficulty without breaking **X**'s confidence... I think I'd better just say no firmly, but also give **B** a positive stroke or two and hope for the best...	
	A. (1) Oh, I'm sorry, **B**... but I'm afraid I can't move either of you at this point. I can see there are difficulties... but I know she likes working with you and you're one of the people the company relies on ... I need you to keep going for the time being.
	B. Well it's not satisfactory... I'll do what I can but I can't vouch for the quality of the work and I'm not sure how long I can last with *X*.
(2) **B**'s a good guy... I know he'll do his best.	**A.** (2) Thanks, **B**. I know you'll do your best.

A's thoughts and words, evaluated in terms of the components of the closed conversation model

Thoughts (1)

'I'm torn between the two of them! I can see **B**'s problem but **X** needs stability...and I can't tell **B** about **X**'s difficulty without breaking X.'s confidence... I think I'd better just say no firmly, but also give **B** a positive stroke or two and hope for the best...'

Characteristic One (We do not question our assumptions). A's assumption is that he cannot do what **B** asks without letting **X** down. It is this that creates his sense of divided loyalties ('I'm torn between the two of them!'), and that obliges him to choose between doing what **B** asks and protecting **X**. In the event *A* chooses to protect *X*.

Characteristic Two (We do not promote partnership). Because **A** has made the decision to refuse **B**'s request for a move, all his energies go into trying to fulfil his own agenda of getting **B** to accept that decision. Therefore, *A* makes up his mind to avoid discussion ('say no firmly').

Characteristic Three (We do not promote the exchange of all relevant information). In order to support his strategy, he decides to make only passing acknowledgment of *B*'s difficulties before making non-relevant comments designed to flatter *B* into acceptance ('... give *B* a positive stroke or two').

Words (1)

> 'Oh, I'm sorry, *B* ... but I'm afraid I can't move either of you at this point. I can see there are difficulties... but I know she likes working with you and you're one of the people the company relies on... I need you to keep going for the time being.'

Closed advocacy (Advocacy is not transparent). *A*'s acknowledgement of *B*'s difficulties is cursory in that he quickly moves on to telling *B* of his decision ('I can't move either of you at this point... I need you to keep going for the time being'). However he gives *B* no reason for his decision and his flattering words ('I know she likes working with you ... you're one of the people the company relies on') are not relevant to *B*'s point and are not illustrated with any evidence. *A* is therefore likely to leave *B* feeling dissatisfied with what is being asked of him.

Closed advocacy (Advocacy without inquiry). *A* states his decision but makes no attempt to elicit *B*'s reaction to it. Thus, unless *B* is inclined to makes a fuss, he may find it difficult to object.

Thoughts (2)

> '*B*'s a good guy... I know he'll do his best.'

Characteristic One (We do not question our assumptions). Concerned as he is with his own need to resolve his conflict of loyalties, *A* only 'hears' *B*'s 'OK... I'll do what I can'. He screens out *B*'s misgivings ('it's not satisfactory... I can't vouch for the quality of the work ... I'm not sure how long I can last with *X*'). *A*'s selective hearing allows him to confirm his view that *B* will accept his decision ('*B*'s a good guy... I know he'll do his best') and that he can ignore his problem.

Characteristic Two (We do not promote partnership). In pursuing his own agenda, *A* does not explore *B*'s obvious misgivings.

Words (2)

'Thanks, *B*. I know you'll do your best.'

Advocacy without Inquiry. A's words ('Thanks, *B*. I know you'll do your best') only respond to *B*'s words of compliance. Because *A* fails to ask a question that explores *B*'s obvious misgivings, his flattering words may come over as evidence that he doesn't really take *B*'s problem seriously.

Summary

A's closed -to-learning thoughts and words prevent his difficulty – a sense of conflicting loyalty to the needs of *B* and *X* – from becoming discussable. As a result *B*'s problem with covering for *X* is not dealt with.

Outcomes

A may feel that he has protected *X* for the present, but he has only done so at the cost of a number of adverse outcomes.

For A. A is likely to be aware that he has not succeeded in dealing with *B*'s difficulty in a satisfactory way.

For A and B's relationship. A's reliance on *B*'s goodwill and the fact that *B*'s concerns have not been dealt with may have a negative effect on *B*'s working relationship with *A*.

For the organisation. The organisation is left with an imbalanced and inefficient working partnership (between *B* and his colleague *X*) that will continue to affect the quality of the work they do.

[For the annotated *open* version of Conversation 6, see Chapter 9, page 177.]

7. Coping with being criticised (closed approach)

A finds it difficult to cope with *B*, a fellow manager, telling him that he (*B*) did not like the way *A* chaired the management meeting.

How might *A* handle his difficulty?

A's thoughts	**A** and **B**'s words
(1) I really find that annoying – I ran the meeting well... but there'll always be someone who'll find something to criticize... well, it'll be his turn to chair the meeting soon and I'll let him know that I'll be watching how he does...	**B**. You know, **A**, I really didn't like the way you chaired the meeting just now. **A**. (1) Oh really, **B**... I felt I ran things pretty well... and I look forward to seeing how you do when it comes to your turn.

A's thoughts and words, evaluated in terms of the components of the closed conversation model

Thoughts (1)

'I really find that annoying – I ran the meeting well... but there'll always be someone who'll find something to criticize... well, it'll be his turn to chair the meeting soon and I'll let him know that I'll be watching how he does...'

Characteristic One (We do not question our assumptions). **A** has an unquestioned assumption ('I ran the meeting well...'). In order to protect this he finds a way of ruling out **B** as a credible critic ('There'll always be someone who'll find something to criticise...'). This dismissive view of **B** recurs with **A**'s assumption that **B** will not do things any better ('...well it'll be his turn to chair the meeting soon...').

Characteristic Two (We do not promote partnership). Because he believes he ran the meeting well and because he negates **B** as a credible critic, **A** does not initiate a discussion about the point that **B** has made. On the contrary, **A** sees **B** as an adversary and seeks to defend himself by delivering a put-down.

Characteristic Three (We do not promote the exchange of all relevant information). Because he believes he ran the meeting well and that **B**'s comments carry no weight, **A** does not ask **B** for the thinking behind his comments.

99

Words (1)

'Oh really, **B**... I felt I ran things pretty well...and I look forward to seeing how you do when it comes to your turn.'

Closed advocacy (Advocacy is not transparent). A makes a judgement ('... I felt I ran things pretty well...') without any supporting evidence that might enable **B** to understand where **A** is coming from. In the absence of supporting evidence, A is likely to come over as high-handed, defensive and not open to any discussion. **A**'s failure to indicate to **B** what kind of thinking lies behind the statement '...and I look forward to seeing how you do...' means that **A**'s words are likely to come over as a put-down. This is likely to deter **B** from getting involved in further discussion.

Closed advocacy (Advocacy without inquiry). A states his own position but makes no inquiry about **B**'s views. This omission is likely to indicate to **B** that A is not interested in his opinion.

Summary

A's unquestioned assumption that he ran the meeting well leads him to structure the exchange in terms of 'attack/defence'. This prevent **B**'s criticism from becoming discussable, and leaves both parties in a stand-off position.

Outcomes

A may see 'winning' over **B** by putting him down, as beneficial. In fact it results in adverse outcomes.

For A. Because A acknowledges no reason to give any further thought to, or to change, the way he chairs meetings, his skills are unlikely to improve.

For A and B's relationship. It is probable that **A** will continue to feel defensive and even hostile towards **B**.

For the organisation. Any problems there may be in meetings as a result of the way A chairs them are not likely to improve. The conversation may also lead to the loss of good working relationships between two of the organisation's managers.

[For the annotated *open* version of Conversation 7, see Chapter 9, page 182.]

8. Responding to non-verbal behaviour that bothers us (closed approach)

A, a trainee manager, is presenting his section plan to *B*, his line manager, when he notices *B* frowning. This raises his anxieties.

How might *A*. deal with his anxiety?

A's thoughts	*A* and *B*'s words
	(*B* frowns as *A* is presenting his section plan.)
(1) *B*'s frowning... that means he doesn't like my plan... that's a bit discouraging... I don't think he realises how well researched it is... I'd better explain that what I'm giving him at the moment is only a summary...	
	A. (1) Of course what I'm giving you is just a summary of my plans... I can assure you each aspect of the plans is thoroughly well researched and I've got all the data here...
	B. I don't think I need to see all of that now.
(2) Oh dear, that sounds like the brush-off... he obviously doesn't like what I'm saying... but I've done all I can... best just leave him with the data... he might appreciate it a bit more when he's had time to look at it more thoroughly.	
	A. (2) Oh, I see. Well, I've given you most of the plan and here's the data... I'll just leave the rest with you...
	B. Oh!... Well... alright then... I'll take it away and get back to you.

A's thoughts and words, evaluated in terms of the components of the closed conversation model

Thoughts (1)

'*B*'s frowning, that means he doesn't like my plan... that's a bit discouraging... I don't think he realises how well researched it is... I'd better explain that what I'm giving him at the moment is only a summary...'

Characteristic One (We do not question our assumptions). A makes an assumption that *B*'s frown means *B* does not like his plan. This is an assumption that worries him, but which he fails to question. It is *A*'s unquestioned assumption that leads him to give a rationale for his plans ('I'd better explain that what I'm giving him at the moment is only a summary').

Characteristic Two (We do not promote partnership). Because he is so sure that he 'reads' *B*'s frown correctly, *A* does not check out what *B* actually thinks. As a result he decides, unilaterally, to try to explain his position.

Characteristic Three (We do not promote the exchange of all relevant information). Although B's frown worries him, A does not raise his worry with B.

Words (1)

'Of course what I'm giving you is just a summary of my plans... I can assure you each aspect of the plans is thoroughly well researched and I've got all the data here...'

Closed advocacy (Advocacy is not transparent). A does not give any reason for his assurances ('I can assure you each aspect of the plans is thoroughly well researched and I've got all the data here...'). Because *B* does not know *A*'s thoughts, *A*'s sudden change of gear (from presenting his plans to defending them) is likely to puzzle him.

Thoughts (2)

'Oh dear, that sounds like the brush-off... he obviously doesn't like what I'm saying... but I've done all I can... best just leave him with the data... he might appreciate it a bit more when he's had time to look at it more thoroughly.'

Characteristic One (We do not question our assumptions). When *B* responds to *A*'s offer of more data ('I don't think I need to see all of that now'), *A* takes this as further confirmation that *B* does not like his plan ('he obviously doesn't like what I'm saying') and that he is being given the brush-off (a further assumption).

Characteristic Two (We do not promote partnership). In response to the perceived 'brush-off', *A* decides to abandon the current presentation without reference to *B*.

Words (2)

> 'Oh, I see. Well, I've given you most of the plan and here's the data... I'll just leave the rest with you...'

Closed advocacy (Advocacy without inquiry). *A* states his intentions ('here's the data... so if I just leave the rest with you...'), but without checking that *B* is happy with what he is suggesting. *B* has been given no access to *A*'s thinking, nor has he been invited to offer his own thoughts.

Summary

A acts on his unquestioned assumption about the meaning of *B*'s frown and breaks off his presentation. *A*'s a result he fails to raise his difficulty – his anxiety about *B*'s response to his presentation – so that it can be discussed.

Outcomes

A's handling of the conversation has a number of adverse outcomes.

For A. Because *A* does not know what *B* thinks of his plans so far, he is left feeling anxious about what *B*'s final verdict might be.

For A and B's relationship. With *A* left uncertain about *B*'s response to his (*A*'s) plan, and *B* possibly puzzled by the abrupt way in which *A* ended the session, the working relationship is not left on a sound footing.

For the organisation. Not only has the task of presenting and discussing *A*'s section plan been interrupted, but *B* has been given more work. All of this may lead to delays and uncertainties in making a decision about the plans.

[For the annotated *open* version of Conversation 8, see Chapter 9, page 185.]

9. Responding to pressure to go beyond what we feel comfortable with (closed approach)

B, a member of staff, asks *A*, a new manager, for advice. *A* knows he is not in a position to give advice that might solve *B*'s difficulty because he knows little concerning the situation about which he is being consulted. However, he feels under pressure to offer advice because he thinks that as a manager he should be in a position to do this.

How might *A* deal with his difficulty?

A's thoughts	*A* and *B*'s words
	B. I've got a problem in the office. Some of the staff are complaining that they are overworked and that others don't pull their weight. I've tried to explain that it only looks that way because the nature of the work varies from person to person. But there's still a lot of tension. Please tell me what to do!
(1) Oh dear! This could be a tricky problem... I wish I knew a bit more about the office... I really don't know about the different jobs or personalities or even how well *B* manages things. But I am *B*'s line manager now and I should be able to support her by giving advice... I'm feeling under pressure here...	
I know, I'll give her some general encouragement and suggest getting involved in some teamwork activities – I remember taking part in that sort of day myself once. It can't do any harm and will give her something to go for.	
	A. (1) Mmmm... Well, you've done the right thing so far. Let's think... how about laying on some kind of bonding activity?
	B. That's a good idea – I've heard of a company that does that sort of thing... but would we be OK for finance?

(2) Oh dear... that's something else I don't know about... but the bonding activity was my idea. I'd better imply that we're likely to have the money. I can always say the budget won't stretch to it if they come up with something really expensive.	
	A. (2) I'm sure we must have a budget for such things... **B**. Great. That gives me hope that the team might come to appreciate each other better

A's thoughts and words, evaluated in terms of the components of the closed conversation model

Thoughts (1)

'Oh dear! This could be a tricky problem... I wish I knew a bit more about the office... I really don't know about the different jobs or personalities or even how well **B** manages things. But I am **B**'s line manager now and I should be able to support her by giving advice... I'm feeling under pressure here...

'I know, I'll give her some general encouragement and suggest getting involved in some teamwork activities – I remember taking part in that sort of day myself once. It can't do any harm and will give her something to go for.'

Characteristic One (We do not question our assumptions). A makes an assumption that he does not question ('I am **B**'s line manager now and I should be able to support **B** by giving her advice'). His unquestioned assumption then puts him under pressure to think up some advice to give to **B**.

Characteristic Two (We do not promote partnership). Because of his assumption, *A* decides, without reference to **B**, how best to 'help' her ('I'll give her some general encouragement... and suggest... teamwork activities... It can't do any harm and will give her something to go for').

Characteristic Three (We do not promote the exchange of all relevant information). A conceals from **B** information about his difficulty in advising her ('I really don't know about the different jobs or personalities or even how well *B* manages things'). Instead, he decides to give *B* encouragement and to offer some rough and ready advice to get involved in teamwork activities.

Words (1)

> 'Mmmm...Well you've done the right thing so far. Let's think... how about laying on some kind of bonding activity?'

Closed advocacy (Advocacy is not transparent). *A* presents his judgement ('Well you've done the right thing so far') as a fact rather than as a personal opinion. Nor does he support this judgement by explaining why *B*'s actions are 'the right thing'. *B* seems reassured by *A*'s confident statement, possibly because it comes from someone of higher status. However, because *A* does not justify his statement, it risks being perceived for what it is – gratuitous encouragement.

Closed inquiry (Inquiry without advocacy). *A*'s question ('... how about laying on some kind of bonding activity?') does not give an adequate basis for *B* to make an informed response since *A* fails to give any reason why a bonding activity might help *B*. (*A*'s lack of understanding of the problem means that he is unable to give an adequate reason.) It is not surprising that *B*, who is desperate to deal with the problem she is facing, agrees to whatever *A* suggests.

Thoughts (2)

> 'Oh dear... that's something else I don't know about... but the bonding activity was my idea. I'd better imply that we're likely to have the money. I can always say the budget won't stretch to it if they come up with something really expensive.'

Characteristic Three (We do not promote the exchange of all relevant information). Though recognising another uncertainty – finance ('that's something else I don't know about'), *A* finds himself planning to give the impression that money would be available ('I'd better imply that we're likely to have the money') and does not think in terms of letting *B* know that his knowledge about the financial situation is limited.

Characteristic Two (We do not promote partnership). *A* unilaterally plans his response to how he will handle things if *B* wants a costly package ('I can always say the budget won't stretch to it if they come up with something really expensive').

Words (2)

'I'm sure we must have a budget for such things....

Closed advocacy (Advocacy is not transparent). *A*'s statement (I'm sure we must have a budget for such things...') lacks the detail that might completely reassure *B*. As a result, these words may come across as vague and uncertain. However, *A*'s status as her line-manager is enough for *B* to feel encouraged by what *A* is saying.

Summary

A's unquestioned assumption that he should offer *B* some advice causes him to offer advice that is ill-informed. It prevents him from making his difficulty – that he doesn't understand the situation well enough to give appropriate advice – from being communicated to *B* and thus being made discussable.

Outcomes

A may see as beneficial the fact that he has come over to *B* as knowing how to handle the situation. However *A*'s approach can be seen to have a number of adverse outcomes.

For A. Because *A* has not disclosed his lack of expertise he runs the risk of giving advice that might backfire and damage his reputation.

For A and B's relationship. If *A*'s advice turns out to be impractical or ineffective, *B* may well feel that *A*'s judgement is poor, thus reducing the likelihood of creating a positive working relationship.

For the organisation. The organisation has to accommodate a manager who does not appear to act within his limitations and a possibility of continuing problems in *B*'s office.

[For the annotated *open* version of Conversation 9, see Chapter 9, page 189.]

10. Handling a conflict of views between ourselves and another person (closed approach)

At a meeting to review allocation of resources, *B,* the Sales Director, puts forward a view that is in complete opposition to the way *A,* the Head of Research and Development, sees things.

How might *A* deal with his difficulty?

A's thoughts	*A* and *B*'s words
	B. I feel that over the next three years the emphasis should shift decisively towards Sales. We should work towards having a significantly greater number of sales people to increase our share of the market.
(1) This makes me so angry. R&D refines and develops the product – without us there wouldn't be anything to sell. If there are extra resources they should come to us, not be siphoned off to Sales.	
Better pay a bit of lip service to Sales so that *B* feels that I value what they do.	
	A. (1) I recognise that we have to sell our products and that your department does a good job… but the most important thing for the company is that we have something to sell that our customers want to buy. That means maintaining and extending the central role played by R&D.
	B. Of course we recognise that we have to have a good product to sell… but it is our sales force who find out what our competitors are up to and what new features customers want. It is us that feed that information back to R&D. With an extended sales force we can get a better overview of the market and a more

	up-to-date one… as well as selling more of our products.
(2) If that happens we'll have ad hoc development in response to market fads and whatever our competitors happen to be doing… steady, fundamental R&D will go out of the window… but better show that I've heard what she's saying so that she believes I can see her side of the argument.	
	A. (2) I agree that the sales force can be a helpful barometer of change and new demands. But we can't have a product development programme that is determined by market whims rather than by sound development principles and expertise. As I said before, that can only happen if R&D at least maintain its current strength and if we increase our numbers.
	B. We view the part R&D plays as very important. But at the end of the day we either sell or we go out of business…and we need more sales people, now, not just to keep our share of the market but to extend it significantly so that we have assured profits over the next few years…

A's thoughts and words, evaluated in terms of the components of the closed conversation model

Thoughts (1)

'This makes me so angry. R&D refines and develops the product – without us there wouldn't be anything to sell. If there are extra resources they should come to us, not be siphoned off to Sales. Better pay a bit of lip service to Sales so that **B** feels that I value what they do.'

Characteristic One (We do not question our assumptions). A makes the assumption that his view is the correct one ('If there are extra resources they should come to us'). Because this assumption is not questioned, it drives A

109

to try to win the argument rather than have a reasoned discussion.

Characteristic Two (We do not promote partnership). **A** plans his moves strategically ('Better pay a bit of lip service to Sales so that **B** feels that I value what they do'). He fails to take on board what **B** is saying. **A** does not make any attempt to involve **B** in deciding how the conversation might best be taken forward. Nor does **A** consider exploring **B**'s position more fully.

Words (1)

'I recognise that we have to sell our products and that your department does a good job... but the most important thing for the company is that we have something to sell that our customers want to buy. That means maintaining and extending the central role played by R&D.'

Closed advocacy (Advocacy is not transparent). **A**'s acknowledgment of **B**'s position ('I recognise that...') is given without any comment that might convince **B** that his acknowledgment is sincere. On the contrary, it is quickly followed by a 'but' and a reassertion of **A**'s own position. Thus **A**'s words are likely to come over as a token acknowledgment of **B**'s views.

Closed advocacy (Advocacy without inquiry). Having put forward his own viewpoint, **A** makes no attempt to check **B**'s reaction to what he has just said, or to explore **B**'s position more fully. This, again, is likely to suggest that **A** is not interested in **B**'s views.

Thoughts (2)

'If that happens we'll have ad hoc development in response to market fads and whatever our competitors happen to be doing... steady, fundamental R&D will go out of the window... but better show that I've heard what she's saying so that she believes I can see her side of the argument.'

Characteristic Two (We do not promote partnership). **A** continues his strategy of plying **B** with more information about his own point of view without either listening to **B** or involving him in genuine discussion.

Words (2)

'I agree that the sales force can be a helpful barometer of change and new demands. But we can't have a product development programme that is determined by market whims rather than by sound

110

development principles and expertise. As I said before, that can only happen if R&D at least maintains its current strength and if we increase our numbers.'

Closed advocacy (Advocacy is not transparent). A repeats the same 'Yes...but' form of words that he used before. ('I recognise that... but we can't have...'). Again, his words are likely to come over as only a token acknowledgment of what *B* has just said. *A* also makes a judgemental reference to 'market whims' without giving any evidence for this judgement. This unsubstantiated viewpoint about something that is central to *B*'s role (the market) is likely to come over as dismissive.

Closed advocacy (Advocacy without inquiry). A continues to advocate his position but fails to inquire into *B*'s reaction to his words or to find out more about *B*'s position. This continues to suggest that *A* is only concerned about his own situation.

Summary

A's unquestioned assumption that his own interests should prevail leads him to assert his own position forcefully in the hope of over-riding *B*. This prevents the underlying difficulty – that they (*A* and *B*) represent different interests – from being identified and made discussable.

Outcomes

A's approach to this conflict of views is likely to produce one of three possible outcomes: a 'win' for *A*, a 'lose' for *A* or a stalemate for *A* and *B*. Even if *A* does achieve a win, this will be only at the cost of adverse consequences for the relationship and for the organisation.

For A. A may 'lose' in that he ends up with an outcome that he finds unacceptable.

For A and B's relationship. The winning of the argument by either A or B (and corresponding bad feeling on the part of the loser) is very likely to have a negative influence on their future working relationship.

For the organisation. Either *A* or *B*'s department will lose out, or the argument will result in a stalemate with continuing rivalry between two important departments. Resources may also be wasted.

[For the annotated *open* version of Conversation 10, see Chapter 9, page 195.]

PART THREE

The Open-to-Learning Approach

6

The Three Principles of Open-to-Learning Thinking

Learning points

A detailed understanding of the three principles of open-to-learning thinking, and how they can have a positive impact on our difficult conversations.

Insight into how we need to change the way we think in order to escape the trap of closed-to-learning thinking and manage difficult conversations more effectively.

~~~~~~~~~~~~~~~~

Through a number of exercises, we invite you to practise thinking in terms of the three open-to-learning principles.

The open-to-learning model: open thinking

In Chapter 2, we presented three aspects of our thinking that we deal with differently, according to whether our approach to a difficult conversation is closed or open. These were: the way we handle our *assumptions*; the extent to which we regard the conversation as a *partnership*; and how we approach the exchange of *information*. We noted that when we are in closed-to-learning mode, which we suggested was the default mode, we fail to question our assumptions, promote partnership or promote the exchange of relevant information. As a result, our approach is ineffective.

In this chapter we explore the three key principles of thinking that is *open*-to-learning. These make up the first part of the open-to-learning model and describe the kind of thinking we need to engage in if we are to make difficulties discussable and handle difficult conversations effectively.

115

We first remind ourselves of the three key principles of open-to-learning thinking:

Principle One:	Question any relevant assumptions
Principle Two:	Promote partnership
Principle Three:	Promote the exchange of all relevant information

We deal with each of these three key principles in turn. We suggest some useful strategies for putting each principle into practice and indicate their positive effects on the conversation.

Principle One:
Question any relevant assumptions

The first principle of open-to-learning thinking (Question any relevant assumptions) is the most important of the three. This is because, in order to engage in open-to-learning thinking, we need to free ourselves from the trap of assumptions that would otherwise go unquestioned. We stand no chance of escaping the limiting effects of closed-to-learning thinking and making our concerns discussable unless we identify and deal with our unquestioned assumptions. However certain we may feel about the truth of our own assumptions, they have the power to misdirect our whole approach to difficult conversations

Therefore, if we are worried about a conversation that could prove difficult or if a conversation 'goes wrong', the first thing we need to do is to question any assumptions we may hold that are relevant to the content or the process of that conversation. We do this in order to be in a position to check whether the assumption is preventing us from making difficulties discussable.

There are two steps involved in ensuring that unquestioned assumptions do not drive us into closed ways of operating. First, we need to identify them as and when they occur. Second, we need to question and deal with them in a way that minimises their potential to prevent us from making difficulties discussable.

The following sections describe some of the steps we need to take to put Principle One into practice.

Step 1. Identify any unquestioned assumptions that may be constraining and misdirecting your approach to the conversation

We need to be checking constantly whether unquestioned assumptions are keeping us closed-to-learning.

A highly effective way of identifying our unquestioned assumptions is to write down our thoughts so that we can look at them objectively, away from the feelings provoked by the difficult conversation concerned and in our own time. This technique can be particularly useful when we want to review an especially difficult conversation, or when we are anticipating one in the near future. Writing down our thoughts not only helps us to identify our unquestioned assumptions, but can also bring into the open unquestioned assumptions that we have not previously been aware of. The evidence from our work is that this method of identifying our assumptions enhances the possibility of real change.

[To appreciate the potential of this way of getting access to our assumptions, we suggest that it would be valuable at this point to carry out at least the first two steps of the Key Exercise, if you have not already done so. Instructions are at the end of Chapters 2 and 3.]

A second way to acquire the skill of spotting our unquestioned assumptions is to practise identifying them in conversations where we are not under the added pressure of having to deal with a difficulty. This is because it is easier to observe ourselves when we are not under stress.

Once we have become skilled at identifying our assumptions, either in retrospect or in the difficult conversations that we anticipate, we will be able to do so while we are actually in the process of a difficult conversation.

Step 2. Deal with your assumptions in a way that minimises their power to constrain your approach

Once we have identified any unquestioned assumptions, we need to prevent them from limiting our thoughts and from keeping us in closed mode.

We have found the following strategies to be useful ways of preventing our assumptions from constraining our approach and enabling us to deal effectively with difficult conversations.

Check the correctness of the assumption

It is often possible to check out the correctness of our assumption with the other person. This increases the chance that the conversation will be conducted on the basis of reality rather than conjecture.

Examples
The unquestioned assumption, 'He's worried', could be tested by, 'I'll ask him if he's worried'.

The unquestioned assumption, 'He doesn't like morning meetings', could be tested by, 'I'll ask him if I'm right in thinking that he doesn't like morning meetings'.

If we are unable to test the correctness of our assumption by checking them out with the other person, an alternative is to observe whether or not our assumption holds true in practice. There are potential pitfalls here. We should be alert to the natural tendency to notice only what we expect to see. A good way to minimise this possibility is to look for any evidence that disconfirms our assumption.

Example
The unquestioned assumption, 'She's always late for meetings', could be tested by, 'I'll try to notice if there are times when she *doesn't* come late for meetings before I say anything about it'.

So strong is our tendency to see only what we are looking for that even if we do not immediately see anything to contradict our assumption, we should continue to keep an open mind.

Example
The unquestioned assumption, 'Her ideas never work', could be replaced by,

'I haven't *so far* been able to find any of her ideas that have worked'.

Put the assumption on one side

If we are not in a position to test the validity of potentially misleading assumptions directly, we should try, for the moment, to put them to one side so that they do not prevent us from having dialogue.

One way of making it easier to put our assumptions on one side is to treat them as possibilities rather than certainties. This can be done by changing words that assume certainty, like 'is' or 'will', into words that indicate uncertainty, like 'may be' or 'might'. Doing so helps to weaken the power of the assumption so that our approach to the conversation can become open-to-learning.

Examples

The unquestioned assumption, 'She's completely wrong', could be replaced by, 'She *may* be wrong'.

The unquestioned assumption, 'If I admit I made a mistake I'll be seen as incompetent', could be replaced by, 'If I admit to a mistake I *won't necessarily* be seen as incompetent'.

Another way of making it easier to put an assumption to one side is to consider an alternative to it. Thus we might try to see things through the eyes of the other person in the conversation. We could also imagine ourselves in the position of a third party who, unlike us, is not influenced by previous experiences of a negative kind.

Examples

If our unquestioned assumption is, 'If I tell my boss what I really think about the new arrangements, I'll be in trouble', possible alternatives might be:

- 'Perhaps my boss would like to hear my views', or
- 'I may be able to present my views in a way that my boss will find acceptable'.

If our unquestioned assumption is, 'This meeting with X is going to be a tricky one', possible alternatives might be:

- 'Maybe X won't react as I expect', or
- 'Maybe there is information about the situation I don't yet have that will make the meeting go differently from the way I expect'.

Once we are able to take the step of questioning our assumptions, we are then able to move from closed-to-learning thinking to open-to-learning thinking. This holds true whether our assumptions are right or wrong.

While Principle One is of fundamental importance in enabling us to open up the *possibility* of making conversational difficulties discussable, it does not assist us in knowing *how* to discuss what needs to be discussed in a way that will be acceptable to both parties. To address this task we also need to think about how to promote partnership (Principle Two) and how to promote the exchange of all information relevant to the conversation concerned (Principle Three).

Principle Two:
Promote partnership

Once we have freed ourselves from any constraints that our unquestioned assumptions might impose on us we are able to think in terms of genuine partnership. If conversations at work are conducted as partnerships they are likely to be beneficial in a number of ways. The idea of partnership encourages us to see interpersonal difficulties as opportunities for joint ways forward rather than as something we have to manage alone. Each person's position then becomes a source of new insights for the other, and from this can emerge fresh perspectives on the difficulty that are helpful to both, identification of common ground and a basis for agreeing a jointly acceptable way forward. Furthermore, a partnership approach enables both parties to feel committed to the outcomes of the conversational process and, for this reason, it is likely to produce durable outcomes.

Although partnership is a two-way process, the task of promoting it has to be our responsibility – as people who have come to understand its importance as a key principle of the open-to-learning model. We cannot rely on the other person to take the initiative. In the following section we therefore look at three main aims that *we* need to pursue in order to help us establish and maintain partnership throughout a difficult conversation. These are:

- Try to ensure that you are both involved in determining the content and direction of the conversation.
- Try to ensure that you stay in touch with one another's thinking throughout the conversation.
- Try to achieve free and informed choices for both parties

Try to ensure that you are both involved in determining the content and direction of the conversation

This can be done in a number of ways as indicated below.

Aim to negotiate agreement about what is to be talked about

> *Examples*
> 'I'll suggest that we start by agreeing our agenda for the phone call.'
> 'I'll ask whether he is prepared to talk about the issue of the budget.'

At the beginning of a conversation, or even during it, if we are able to negotiate agreement on what is to be talked about, we will both be more committed to discussion of the topic concerned. We will also feel more confident that our own concerns can be voiced during that discussion.

Promote the identification of shared goals

Partnership is promoted when both parties work towards jointly agreed goals.

Examples
'I'll try and sort out what it is we are both aiming at.'
'How can we get the best for our clients while at the same time making sure that neither of us is overloaded with work.'

Working towards shared goals is particularly effective if we are at loggerheads with the other person.

Example
In the open version of Conversation 10 (page 195), there is conflict between the Head of Research and Development and the Sales Director about whose department should receive additional resources. The Head of Research and Development thinks of getting past the impasse by following the line, 'I'm thinking in terms of "I'm right. She's wrong". It's possible that both our views are valid and that what we need is a way forward that will take account of both our points of view.'

Promote agreement about how to proceed in the conversation

In a difficult conversation, we may feel uncertain about how to proceed, or have a sense that things are somehow going wrong. Sharing such perceptions with the other person, rather than unilaterally making a decision about how to manage the conversation, makes the responsibility for its conduct a mutual one and minimises the risk of perpetuating the difficulties.

Examples
'I'm not sure how best to give her feedback. I'll ask her where she would like to start.'

'I feel as though the conversation is going round in circles. I'll let him know that I've got a problem and see if we can work out how to move forward from there.'

There are occasions when it may be necessary for one of the participants to speak at some length about an issue or concern. However, if an open-to-

121

learning approach is to be maintained, it is important to seek the other person's agreement to listen to any lengthy contribution we may wish to make, as well as to signal our willingness to listen to an extended comment by the other person.

If we do find that one person is doing all the talking without the explicit agreement of the other, it is important to address the issue openly.

Examples
'I'll let him know I need to interrupt him because...'
'I feel as though I've been doing all the talking. I'll encourage him to let me know his position.'

Ensure that your own preferred outcome does not prevent partnership

To sustain a difficult conversation as a partnership may sometimes require us to let go of an outcome that we had in mind before the conversation began, in order to free us to negotiate outcomes that are jointly acceptable.

Example
In the closed version of Conversation 10 (page 108), the Head of R&D has to let go of his own preferred outcome (that resources should come to his department rather than to Sales) in order to make discussion and thus negotiation possible.

Nevertheless, on some occasions, a conversation might need to be about outcomes that have been decided beforehand and which cannot be negotiated, even though one party may regard such outcomes as adverse. For example, we may have to communicate to the other person a ruling that has already been made, such as a change in the membership of their team, the early stages of grievance or disciplinary procedures or a move of location. Even so, by sustaining the conversation as a partnership, the other person, however much they might dislike its *content*, is very likely to find the *process* of the conversation acceptable. This increases our chance of maintaining good working relationships throughout the conversation, as well as afterwards.

Example
In Conversation 2 (page 161), a manager focuses on making the news of a member of staff's (non-negotiable) relocation and, especially her reaction to it, discussable. As a result, although the member of staff may not like what she is told, she is likely to feel that, within the constraints of the situation, her manager has been able to say what he had to say and, at the same time, has made the process of the conversation acceptable. The working relationship is thus maintained.

Try to ensure that you stay in touch with one another's thinking throughout the conversation

For our conversation to be a partnership, each of us needs to know and understand the other's thinking throughout the conversation. This ensures that our discussion rests on agreed foundations. There are a number of ways in which we might do this.

Aim to check that you both understand what the other person is saying

It is important that our understanding of the other person and their understanding of us are explicitly and regularly checked out. In this way, any confusion can be clarified as it arises and serious misunderstandings minimised.

Examples

'I need to check that I have understood correctly what he wants me to do.'

'I'm not very clear about that last point – I'd better ask her to explain it again.'

'I'm not sure he's following me – I'll check what he understands me to have said.'

Aim to probe any doubts or hesitations the other person may have about a suggested course of action, and express any doubts or hesitations of your own

Sometimes people feel reluctant to express doubts and hesitations about a course of action that is being suggested. This can lead to decisions being made which do not have the support they seem to have. Dealing explicitly with doubts and hesitations maximises the chance that decisions will be informed by people's actual thoughts and feelings.

Examples

'He seems to be uncertain. I'll check whether my idea is likely to create any difficulties for him.'

'I need to let her know that I'm not really happy with what she is suggesting.'

Aim to check whether the other person goes along with what you say, and let them know whether or not you go along with what they say

It is important that we think in terms of making both disagreements and agreements explicit so that we are able to move forward together on the basis of knowing where we both stand.

Examples
'I'll ask him what he thinks about what I've just said.'
'I'll ask him if he agrees with what I'm saying.'
'I'll let her know that I don't agree with what she is saying.'
'I'll let her know that I don't agree with what she is saying.'

In our discussion of closed-to-learning thinking, we saw how seldom most of us try to find out whether the other person agrees or disagrees with us, or whether or not they share our concerns. If we always have it in mind to follow through our comments by inviting the other person to respond to what we have just said, this will make it far more likely that the conversation becomes a partnership. It also makes it more difficult for the other person to ignore what we say and to pursue their own agenda.

Conversely, where the other person is operating in closed-to-learning mode, it is unlikely that they will ask for our response. Thus, we should take on the responsibility of responding openly and directly to what the other person says.

Even when we do not go along with what the other person is saying, it is important to remember to acknowledge their position. This is particularly true when we realise that the other person is trying to communicate a difficulty they have. Acknowledging that they have a difficulty (even if at first we do not fully understand it) lets them know that we accept it as a basis for further discussion.

Example
In the extended conversation between a headteacher and a Head of Science in Chapter 10 (page 202), the headteacher thinks to herself, 'His (point of view) is a fair one', even though she herself sees things differently. She therefore decides to let the Head of Science know that she accepts what he is saying in order to signal that they have some common ground from which to negotiate.

Try to achieve free and informed choices for both parties

We need to aim for free and informed choice so that neither person in the conversation feels coerced into a position they do not want to be in. There are a number of ways in which we can promote this aim.

Regard one another as equals

In a work setting, we often have to engage in a difficult conversation with someone of different status. A prerequisite of being able to think in terms of free and informed choices is that we regard ourselves and the other person as equals, irrespective of status or expertise. This does not mean that either of us needs to abdicate our designated roles within the organisation. What it does mean is that the rights and responsibilities associated with those roles are amongst the factors that inform the conversation, but that neither person's contribution is seen as superior or inferior to that of the other.

Example
In the open version of Conversation 5 (page 173), in spite of a difference in status, a hard-pressed junior manager decides to appeal to their respective responsibilities to get her unheeding senior manager to listen to her concerns. 'He's still not hearing me... I think I've got to let him know that it's not just my problem... it affects him as well,because some of the work just won't get done... and give him a choice as to who decides.'

Offer an informed choice to the other person, and claim the opportunity to make an informed choice for yourself

In offering and claiming choice, our task is to ensure that the information needed is available for making choices that are well founded. This may include such matters as data about our respective positions on the subject being discussed, factual information about organisational constraints on the choices available to us, or the likely consequences of any decisions we make.

Examples
'I need to explain both options and make my own preferences clear so that he can make his own decision in the light of these.'

'I'll tell him that I have both good news and bad news and ask him which he'd like to hear first.'

'I'll tell him I would like to know more of the background to his suggestion before I commit myself.'

'She's assuming that I'm prepared to be phoned at home. I need to make it clear that I'm not happy with that unless it's urgent.'

Give the other person choice over decisions intended to protect them, and claim your own choice in decisions intended to protect you

When we perceive other people as having some sort of personal difficulty (or we ourselves are in difficulties), it is easy to take a unilateral decision about whether, or how, to 'protect' them. In practice, however, the other person may not find the decision we make helpful. Therefore, if we want to respond to the other person's need appropriately, it is important that we first check their wishes. Similarly, if we feel the other person is trying to protect us against our wishes, we should let them know what those wishes are.

> *Examples*
> 'He seems to find walking difficult, but I'll check with him first before reserving a parking space for him near the building.'
>
> 'I feel that colleagues are skirting round my personal issues. I'll let them know that I'd welcome the chance to talk about what's been happening at home.'

Sometimes painful feelings arise in the course of a conversation. From the point of view of partnership, it is important that neither person in a conversation is obliged to handle more than they feel able to cope with. We should encourage the communication of any painful feelings so that there is the opportunity to make a joint decision about how best to deal with them. (We say more about this way of dealing with our feelings under Principle Three.)

> *Examples*
> 'He's looking a bit upset... I should check... and if he is upset, ask him if he wants me to go on.'
>
> 'I'm finding her feedback very discouraging. We need to agree that I can let her know when I've had enough.'

Principle Three:
Promote the exchange of all relevant information

This section looks at the third key principle of open conversation, 'Promote the exchange of all relevant information'. This principle is closely linked to the previous one in that it is very difficult to promote partnership (Principle Two) unless both parties in a conversation are working on the basis of information that is shared. In difficult conversations, putting relevant information 'on the table' makes such sharing possible.

To count as 'relevant', information must be related to the topic being discussed. It must also enable the listener to interpret correctly what is being said, and to gauge the status of that information – what validity and worth it has. The listener is then in a position to decide for themselves in what way they wish to make use of the information offered.

Below we look at two aims that will help us promote the exchange of all relevant information. These are:

- Try to ensure that all relevant information is on the table.
- Try to make clear the status of anything you say or ask.

Try to ensure that all relevant information is on the table

We can do this in a number of ways.

Make sure that there are not any 'no-go' areas of difficulty for discussion

Sometimes people are well aware of difficulties that are relevant to their work but are afraid to raise them for discussion. However, such difficulties could undermine our well-being at work unless we bring them into the open and make them discussable.

Examples
'If we are going to work together, I feel we need to discuss some of the difficulties we've been having in getting on with each other, however difficult we may find that.'

'Colleagues are tiptoeing around the problem of *X*'s attitude. I'll suggest that we talk to *X* openly about the difficulties we are having so that there's a chance of resolving the problem.'

Be prepared to make explicit any difficulties you have that result from the other person's actions

We frequently fail to make explicit difficulties we are having as a result of something the other person in the conversation has said or done, either before or during the conversation. Instead, negative feelings may be expressed through our tone of voice, body language, or by remaining silent. This can lead to the other person misinterpreting or ignoring our signals and to losing the opportunity to sort out the difficulties. Being explicit about our difficulties increases the likelihood that the other person will register that we have a problem. It enables us to open up our difficulties for discussion, so that we stay open-to-learning and the conversation remains effective.

Thinking of a difficulty in terms of the problem that we experience enables us to present it as *our* problem (rather than apportioning blame). It also minimises the chance that the other person will prevent effective discussion by reacting defensively.

Examples
'I need to let her know that when she won't speak to her colleagues I have a major problem in my role as her manager.'

'When he next arrives late for a meeting with me, I'll let him know that it's difficult to use the time while I'm waiting for him and that this causes me a problem.'

Be prepared to communicate and acknowledge feelings that have implications for the conversation, and encourage the other person to do the same

When our feelings are likely to affect what we think and say in a difficult conversation, information about those feelings becomes relevant to the discussion. It is therefore very important to communicate those feelings and the reasons for them to the other person. A good way to do this is to describe our feelings in factual terms – that is, in the same way that we would give any other kind of information. Similarly, if we are concerned about how the other person might be feeling, we can ask them to tell us.

Examples
'I can feel myself getting anxious as she describes her plans because they're not what I expected... I'll let her know how I feel so that we can talk about it.'

'I'm not sure how the organisational changes have left her feeling. That's making it difficult for me to talk to her about them. Best thing is to ask her straight out how she feels.'

Be prepared to make clear the likely consequences of a refusal to discuss a difficulty

One of the hardest things to deal with in a relationship is when another person refuses to discuss with us a difficulty that we have and in which they are implicated. When we meet a blank wall of this kind, the best we can do is to ensure that the other person is in a position to make the choice whether or not to discuss the problem in the light of adequate information about the likely consequences if they refuse to discuss the issue openly.

Communicating this kind of information can be very helpful both to the process and to the content of the conversation. It is also the kind of information that we may not always think of giving. Notice that the information offered should not be a threat, but a clearly stated indication of the only option(s) available if the other person will not discuss the issue with us, which they might need to consider.

Examples
'He needs to know that if he is not willing to discuss this issue I can see no choice but to raise my problem with his line manager.'

'She may not realise that if she is not willing to discuss amendments to this letter I will not be able to support what she has written. That's something I need to tell her.'

'I need to let her know that if she dismisses my views out of hand it is going to make it very difficult for us to work together.'

[For an annotated example of making clear the likely consequences, see the open version of Conversation 5 on page 173.]

Try to make clear the status of anything you say or ask

We highlight below the kind of information we should be ready to give in order to help the other person to assess the status (the validity or worth) of what we say. They may need this kind of information in order to be able to make this assessment. If the other person does not give us this kind of information, we should ask for it.

Be prepared to give the reasoning behind what you say or ask, and any background data

We should always be prepared to give the reasoning and any background data on which we base what we say. This enables the other person to interpret and assess our words accurately so that they are able to respond in an informed way. It also enables them to challenge the reasoning and the data itself.

Examples
'I will tell him that the reason why I'm saying that X needs to know what is being proposed is because X will be affected by the decision.'

129

'I must make sure he realises that my advice is based on government statistics.'

'I must make it clear that the reason I'm suggesting that she no longer works on her own is because I'm concerned about her safety.'

The same preparedness to give background data is true when we ask a question.

Examples
'When I ask him if he will be in the office tomorrow morning, I need to explain that I'm hoping that he can take a phone call for me...otherwise he may think I'm wanting him to stand in for me.'

'When I ask her how many absences she's had this year, I need to make it clear that I'm asking because I have to fill in a return sheet... otherwise she may see the question as implying criticism.'

If the other person is uncertain why we are asking a question, they may feel they are being manipulated and be wary of giving a straight answer. If we give the thinking behind the question, understanding will be enhanced and we are likely to get an informed response.

Be prepared to make the origins of your statements or questions explicit

Making explicit the origins of our statements or questions, and whose view it is that we are expressing, is also part of the information we should be prepared to give in order that the other person can assess the status of what we are saying. Conversely, if we do not make clear the origins of what we are saying, we run the risk of creating misunderstanding or defensiveness.

Examples
'I'll say that we should go ahead but let him know that this is my own personal view.'

'I'll let him know that the comment I just made comes from what the consultant said in his report.'

'I'll let her know that it's at the team's request that I am asking about leave arrangements.'

Be prepared to give the reasoning and/or supporting evidence for any evaluative comments you make, and request similar evidence for any evaluative comments the other person makes

When we make an evaluative comment the most helpful kind of supporting evidence is data that is verifiable, because this allows evidence to be checked and discussed by both parties. In order to do this we need to be alert to the finding (Argyris 1992 p.14) that our natural tendency is to make statements that are based on inference, rather than being based directly on the observable data itself.[8]

Examples

'I'll reassure my line manager that Mr T is a reliable colleague... for one reason, that he has met all last year's deadlines.'

'I need to find out exactly what he was referring to when he said my work was of poor quality.'

On some occasions we may find that we cannot easily identify supporting evidence for a judgement we want to make. When this happens we may need, for the sake of exchanging valid and relevant information, to suspend judgement or, alternatively, make it clear to the other person that we have not been able to verify the evidence on which our judgement is based.

Using the three principles of open-to-learning thinking interactively

The focus and direction of any of our difficult conversations tends to shift as the conversation progresses, and it can be difficult to know which of the principles to apply at any moment. Although, for the purposes of illustration, we have dealt with them in a particular order, the three principles can be used in whatever way we find helpful at the time.

No single principle by itself can enable us to manage difficult conversations effectively. All three need to inform and guide our thinking. While Principle One (Question any relevant assumptions) is essential in enabling us to escape the danger of closed-to-learning thinking that will prevent us making difficulties discussable, we need Principle Two (Promote partnership) and Principle Three (Promote the exchange of all relevant

---

[8] Argyris' concept of a 'ladder of inference' details this tendency, and is briefly described in Appendix A.

information) to guide our thinking as to *how* to make previously undiscussable difficulties discussable.

The point is that we need to recognise that the three principles are interactive. If, for example, during the conversation, we have difficulty in thinking in terms of Principles Two or Three, there may be a need to look again for any unquestioned assumptions (Principle One)

In the next chapter we will be looking at how the forms of words we use are informed by, and can express, the three principles of open-to-learning thinking.

Exercises to help you put the three principles of open-to-learning thinking into practice

Principle One: Question any relevant assumptions

- In difficult conversations at work, try to be aware of the times when you make unquestioned assumptions about what the other person is saying or about how they are behaving. Try out alternative interpretations (however unlikely you may think these to be) in order to practise the art of seeing things from a different perspective.

- Identify a forthcoming conversation at work that you think will prove difficult. Write down your thoughts and feelings about how you think the conversation will go. Let your thoughts flow and try not to censor them. Then underline any assumptions you have made that could determine the way you approach the conversation. Before going into the conversation remind yourself of these assumptions. During the conversation, make a deliberate effort to stop them determining your approach. Either check their validity with the other person, or put them on one side for the time being, so that you are free to make the discussion a partnership.

Principle Two: Promote partnership

- Think of an argument or difference of opinion at work that you have had recently. Review the conversation and try to identify any joint goals that you might have focused on.

- Practise giving choices to others in everyday situations where you may not always do so. For example:
  - Checking others' preferences before adjusting the heating.
  - Finding out, when you phone another person, whether this a convenient time for them.

- Practise seeing interpersonal difficulties as an opportunity for inviting discussion and a co-operative approach to solving problems.

Principle Three: Promote the exchange of all relevant information

- Be alert to any uncomfortable feelings that you may have before or during a conversation. If you sense that these feelings are influencing the discussion in a negative way, state your feelings as factually as you can and give the reasons for them.

- If you believe that another person has undisclosed feelings that are preventing conversational difficulties being dealt with effectively, check out your perception with them and, if necessary, encourage a joint decision about how best to handle the situation.

- Practise giving the other person information that will help them assess the validity of what you say. Let them know when your statement is a personal opinion (for example, by prefacing what you say by 'I think' or 'In my view') and make your reasoning explicit.

- If you find yourself in a situation where someone continues to refuse to discuss an issue with you, consider letting them know the likely consequences of their refusal. To help you identify these consequences ask yourself the following kind of questions:

  o What would I (or others) be likely to do next if there is a refusal to discuss, and why?
  o How might this affect the other person?
  o What effect will refusal to discuss have on our working relationship?

Key exercise step 4:

Revising your thoughts in terms of the open-to-learning model

Instructions for Step 4 of the Key Exercise are to be found in Appendix B under the heading '**Revising your thoughts in terms of the open-to-learning model**' (page 247). This will guide you to evaluate your thoughts, in the difficult conversation you recorded in Step 1, in terms of the three principles of the open-to-learning thinking described in this chapter.

7

The Forms of Words that Express Open-to-Learning Thinking

Learning points

A detailed understanding of the forms of words that express open-to-learning thinking.

How open forms of words make difficulties discussable in a way that is acceptable to both participants.

Insight into how we need to change the forms of words we use in order to make our approach to difficult conversations more effective.

~~~~~~~~~~~~~~~~

Through a number of exercises, we invite you to practise using forms of words that express your open-to-learning thinking in what you say.

The open-to-learning model: open forms of words

In the last chapter, we looked at the sort of *thinking* that is essential if we are to manage difficult conversations in ways that are effective. This chapter is about the second part of the open-to-learning model, with the focus on how we can ensure that the *forms of words* we use in our conversations reflect the principles of open-to-learning thinking.

Questioning any relevant assumptions (Principle One) frees us to say what we really want or need to say and respond to what the other person is trying to communicate. At the same time, being concerned to promote partnership (Principle Two) and to exchange all relevant information (Principle Three), will lead to us using open forms of words (open advocacy and open inquiry) that result in difficulties becoming discussable and the conversation having beneficial outcomes.

The effects of open-to-learning thinking on advocacy and inquiry

In order to express thinking that is open-to-learning, we need to use advocacy and inquiry in ways that are different from when our thinking is closed. We need to use them in ways that are open. We remind ourselves that 'advocacy' refers to those statements we make that convey information about the way we see things – our wishes, views, concerns or feelings. Advocacy may also communicate relevant background reasoning and information relevant to these wishes, views, concerns or feelings. 'Inquiry' refers to questions we ask that seek to elicit information about the other person's ideas, wishes, opinions, feelings or problems. Inquiry also includes requests for factual information relevant to the other person's viewpoint or situation.

In this chapter we look at what we mean by *open* advocacy and *open* inquiry.

Open advocacy

Advocacy is open when our words express our open-to-learning thinking. They do so when our 'advocacy is transparent' and when it is accompanied by inquiry – 'advocacy with inquiry'.

Advocacy is transparent

Many of the statements we make when we advocate our point of view are interpretations, theories or conclusions rather than verifiable facts. We can make our advocacy transparent, and thus express our open-to-learning thinking in our words, by including the kind of information that enables listeners to assess whether or not such statements are true or reasonable, and to comment on the steps that have led us to our conclusions. We illustrate some ways of doing this below.

Communicate your reasoning and give your evidence when you express a view about a particular situation or make an evaluative comment about an individual or their performance

Examples:
'There's no point in going ahead because we will overrun the budget', rather than, 'There's no point in going ahead'.

'It's not a job for her because the client has a history of attacking women', rather than, 'It's not a job for a woman'.

Phrases like 'as we will overrun the budget' or 'because the client has a history of attacking women', give the other person access to the thinking behind statements that express inferences and opinions ('there's no point in going ahead', 'I don't think it's a job for her [as a woman]'). Offering such background information minimises the likelihood that the other person will have to guess at, and possibly misinterpret, why we are expressing a particular view.

When we express a view about another person, it is important to give our evidence. If we are unable to be transparent in this way, it may be that we should either not state our view or we should rethink it. The most helpful kind of evidence is specific and accurate, rather than vague or exaggerated.

Example:
'Mr S is unreliable because he was late with two out of his last three deadlines', rather than, 'Mr S is unreliable'.

So, in the case of the example above, 'because he was late with two out of his last three deadlines' is better than 'because he is late with his deadlines', which, in turn, is better than 'Mr S is unreliable'. The more specific our supporting evidence, the more the other person is given the means of making an informed judgement about the validity of our view. 'Because he was late with two out of his last three deadlines' allows the other person to disagree with our opinion that being late with two out of three deadlines signals unreliability. This leaves the door open to explore possible explanations for Mr S's lateness other than 'unreliability'.

If we want to express a view about the person we are talking to we should give supporting evidence that is specific and verifiable. This allows the other person to understand and comment on the reason for our opinion, rather than being faced with only our conclusion. In this way we maximise the possibility of the other person giving a reasoned response and, where the view is negative, not becoming defensive or hostile.

Examples:
'This report is unsatisfactory because you did not follow the guidelines provided', rather than, 'This report is unsatisfactory'.

'That was a good presentation because you held people's interest with the examples you used', rather than, 'That was a good presentation'.

In the case of the first example above (concerning an unsatisfactory report), the speaker achieves two things. He uses evidence ('because you did not follow the guidelines') that can be verified. He also creates an opportunity for the other person to correct any misunderstanding. Because the listener knows what the speaker regards as evidence for their view, the listener is in a position to respond with such words as, 'I didn't know there were any guidelines', or, 'I found the guidelines very difficult to follow'.

Make clear whose opinion is being expressed

Examples
'In my view there's no point in going ahead', rather than, 'There's no point in going ahead'.

'The consultant's opinion was that the management structure needs reorganising', rather than, 'The management structure needs reorganising'.

There are times when it is important for us to make clear whose opinion is being expressed, as with 'In my view' or 'The consultant suggested' above. This enables the other person to come to an informed judgment about how seriously to take the remark or with whom to explore it further.

Use words that communicate your ownership of your difficulty

Example
'I've got a problem ....I find myself getting irritated when you interrupt me', rather than, 'You irritate me when you interrupt'.

When we want to communicate a problem we are experiencing, it is helpful if we couch it in terms of personal ownership. 'I've got a problem...when...', rather than laying the blame – explicitly or implicitly – on another person. In the example above the speaker takes responsibility for the difficulty, offers more information and is less likely to be perceived as accusatory than if they simply say something like, 'You irritate me when you interrupt'. To own a difficulty is more likely to encourage a positive response than create a defensive reaction, particularly if we follow up our ownership with an inquiry such as, 'Would it be OK to talk about my difficulty?'

Similarly, where the difficulty is the result of a conflict of views, it is helpful to use 'we' language that indicates a shared problem, before clarifying where opinions differ.

Example
'I think we have a problem here. I believe you think X, whereas I think Y.'

We are not suggesting that our statements should always be accompanied by exhaustive explanation. The important thing is that we give *enough* background information to minimise the possibility of the other person failing to understand or misinterpreting our reasons for saying what we say, and to maximise the possibility of a useful and appropriate response. Giving appropriate reasoning and evidence in the ways indicated above also enables the other person to challenge the basis of our interpretations, theories or conclusions. We can use such responses to test, inform and modify our own assumptions as necessary. All of this helps us to remain open-to-learning, keeps difficulties discussable and contributes to resolving problems.

Advocacy with inquiry

By 'advocacy with inquiry' we mean that when we express a viewpoint or make a comment (advocacy), we need to check the other person's response to that statement with a question (inquiry). Checking the other person's response to our advocacy is, in itself, a powerful way of communicating both transparency and genuineness.

Advocacy with inquiry reflects Principle Two in that it promotes partnership through our regularly checking that we understand one another as the conversation progresses. It also reflects the need to exchange relevant information (Principle Three) in that it helps to elicit information that may otherwise not have been forthcoming and that might lead us to modify our views.

Link your statements to a question that checks the other person's response to what you say

It is often necessary explicitly to ask the other person how they respond to what we have just said, rather than assuming or simply hoping that they understand or share our views.

Examples

'I've explained what I think has been going on *(advocacy...)*. Did my explanation make sense to you *(...with inquiry)*?'

'I want to start our discussion by telling you what was said on the course I went to *(advocacy...)*. Do you feel this would be a useful starting point *(...with inquiry)*?'

'I'm assuming that because of your health problems you'd prefer a ground floor office' *(advocacy...)*. Am I right about that *(...with inquiry)*?'

Relate your question directly to the statement that has been made

Advocacy with inquiry can best fulfil the purpose of eliciting valid feedback if the question relates directly to the statement that has been made. We can see this most clearly if we compare three kinds of question a speaker might use in order to feel comfortable about leaving a meeting to take a phone call. In each case his advocacy (but not his inquiry) is the same. Only the third is an example of what we mean by advocacy with inquiry.

Question 1

'I'm going to have to leave the meeting at some point to take a phone call *(advocacy)*... Don't you think this room is very stuffy *(inquiry not related to preceding advocacy)*?'

In this example the question is asked to elicit a reply about the room rather than one concerning the speaker's need to leave the meeting.

Question 2

'I'm going to have to leave the meeting at some point to take a phone call *(advocacy)*... Can I use your office, chairman *(inquiry not related to advocacy)*?'

In this example, advocacy and inquiry are again unrelated, but in a way that is less obvious. The speaker's question is asking for feedback on something not directly related to his preceding statement. This is not what we mean by advocacy with inquiry.

Question 3
'I'm going to have to leave the meeting at some point to take a phone
call *(advocacy)*. Is that OK with everyone *(inquiry related to
advocacy)*?'

This is an example of genuine advocacy with inquiry. The inquiry, 'Is that
OK with everyone?', is designed to check out the response of colleagues to
the speaker's initial statement. This inquiry encourages the speaker's
colleagues to let him know how they feel about his intentions. He is,
therefore, likely to learn how best to handle the situation when the phone
call comes.

Advocacy and inquiry do not have to be separated out, but can be made
in a single sentence and in any order. Inquiry does not have to be explicit
but can occur non-verbally through our intonation or, for example, by
simply raising our eyebrows to indicate that we're asking a question.

When our advocacy communicates a difficulty, a particularly useful type
of follow-up inquiry is to invite the other person to discuss the difficulty.
Such questions communicate a genuine intent to see them as a partner in the
conversation. Issuing such an invitation greatly increases our chances of
making difficulties discussable, compared to when we simply advocate our
own position.

Examples
'I'm having a problem at home that is affecting my work. Can we talk
about it?'

'I'm finding it difficult to concentrate when you are on the phone. Can
we try and sort it out?'

As we noted earlier in the chapter, the use of 'we' rather than 'I' (as in 'Can
we talk about it?') is particularly helpful in this kind of inquiry.

Advocacy with inquiry is all about creating partnership. Giving the other
person access to our own position whilst checking their response with
explicit and appropriate questions helps the participants to focus on and deal
with one point at a time. This promotes shared understandings at each step
of the conversation and ensures that it remains relevant to both parties. By
advocating and inquiring, one step at a time, we prevent the escalation of
misunderstandings, unresolved disagreements and divergent agendas that

are the hallmark of conversations that go wrong and cause us so much stress.

Open inquiry

Inquiry is open when it expresses our open-to-learning thinking in what we say. It is open when 'inquiry is genuine' and when it is accompanied by advocacy – 'inquiry with advocacy'.

Inquiry is genuine

To be open, inquiry should have genuine information-seeking intent. When our requests for information are genuine, we are much more likely to get the feedback we need to test our ideas and views. Questions that offer a genuine choice of reply, rather than being gratuitous or coercive, promote partnership through free and informed choice (Principle Two). They serve to promote the exchange of relevant information (Principle Three) by helping to bring to the surface thoughts and wishes that the other person may have, but feels unable to disclose unless invited to.

However, in order to benefit from the genuineness of our questions, the other person needs to perceive that they do in fact have a choice of reply. This raises the issue of how we can make the fact that a question is genuine, clear to the other person. Here are some suggestions.

Make sure that the non-verbal signals that accompany your questions reflect your information-seeking intention

Examples

'Are we all in agreement?' accompanied by a careful look round at the whole group, rather than, 'So we're all agreed, aren't we?' accompanied by a quick glance that signals a wish to move immediately to the next item on the agenda.

'Would you like to think it over?' accompanied by an enquiring look at the other person and giving time for a reply, rather than immediately moving on to another topic.

Indicate that you are equally prepared for a 'Yes' or 'No' answer

Example

'Are we all in agreement? Please do say if you don't agree.'

'Would you like to think the matter over?... Or if you've already made a decision, it would be helpful to know what it is.'

A good way to test whether or not our inquiry is genuine is to ask ourselves whether we are prepared to take on board not only replies that confirm our views but responses that may challenge them.

Example
'Can you stand in for me at tomorrow's meeting?' is not a genuine inquiry if, whatever their answer, we intend the other person to stand in for us.

Inquiry with advocacy

By inquiry with advocacy we mean that when we ask a question, we make clear our reasons for asking it.

Inquiry with advocacy reflects the principles of open-to-learning thinking. It is about working in partnership (Principle Two) in that it helps to ensure a shared understanding of any questions that are asked. This significantly reduces the chance of the other person misinterpreting our question. In giving the other person access to the thinking behind our question, inquiry with advocacy also furthers the exchange of relevant information (Principle Three). Giving our reasons for asking a question will also enable the listener to feel that our inquiry is genuine.

When you ask a question make clear why you are asking

Examples
'Are you thinking of staying in the office this afternoon *(inquiry...)?* I'm asking because I wondered if you could take a phone call for me *(...with advocacy)*', rather than, 'Are you thinking of staying in the office this afternoon *(inquiry alone)?*'.

'Are you the homeowner *(inquiry...)?* I'm asking because my brief is to deal with homeowners only *(...with advocacy)*', rather than, 'Are you the homeowner *(inquiry alone)?*'.

Sometimes it is helpful to put advocacy before the inquiry in order that the inquiry, when it comes, is already in context.

Example
'I've been very worried about you *(advocacy...)*. Where have you been *(...inquiry)?*, rather than, 'Where have you been *(inquiry alone)?*'.

We are more likely to get an answer that relates directly to our question if we give our reasons for asking it. It avoids the other person being placed in the position of having to guess why we are asking our question and offers them an informed choice in making their response. Like advocacy with inquiry, inquiry with advocacy enables us to bring together the contributions of both speaker and listener, to address difficulties as they occur and thus prevent misunderstandings escalating.

Exercises for practising advocacy and inquiry that express open-to-learning thinking

Advocacy is transparent

- When you offer a personal opinion *(advocacy)*, practise making it clear to the other person that what you say is your opinion not a statement of fact. If you are unsure, whether the other person's view is also a personal one, inquire about it. Do you find that being clear about the basis of what is said (personal opinion or objectively verifiable data) helps to make difficulties discussable?

- Practise being alert to those thoughts that the other person might need to know in order to understand what you say. It may be sufficient to give an outline of your ideas or views *(advocacy)* but be prepared to offer the other person further information if they request it. In terms of promoting partnership, it can help both parties to remain actively involved if information is exchanged one point at a time, with ongoing checking to see whether more information is needed or not.

- Be alert to any evaluative comment you make *(advocacy)* – positive or negative – especially when it relates to other people. Make sure that you are in a position to offer the type of evidence that will enable the listener to evaluate it for themselves.

- Practise letting the other person know your reaction *(advocacy)* to what they say – in particular whether or not you understand or agree with the points they are making. This helps to ensure that you are both in a good position to sort out any differences that arise as the conversation progresses. It also means your discussion of difficult issues is more likely to develop into a working partnership *(Principle Two)*.

Advocacy with inquiry

- In any conversation at work, practise checking that the other person understands and/or agrees with what you say, for example asking, 'Do you see it that way?' or 'Does that make sense to you?'
  Note how you sometimes get an unexpected answer. Note also how inquiry with advocacy can open up a conversation and send it in a new and helpful direction.

- If you have a concern about something another person has done or said but are not sure how to tell them, try out the following routine which links advocacy with inquiry:

  o **Step 1: Advocacy**
  Describe the words or behaviour that create a problem for you.

  Example
  '*B*, when I'm working you often chat to me.'

  o **Step 2: Advocacy continued**
  State why these words or behaviour are a problem for you.

  Example
  'That creates a problem for me because it distracts me from what I'm trying to do.'

  o **Step 3: Inquiry**
  Check the other person's reaction by inquiring about the accuracy of your perception and/or whether or not the other person agrees that the consequences of their words or behaviour are problematic.

  Example
  'Can you see my difficulty?'

Inquiry is genuine

- Before asking a question that offers the other person a choice, prepare yourself for whatever answer they might give, especially if it is an answer you might not want. If you find yourself resisting a particular response from the other person, reflect on whether your question was a genuine one.

Inquiry with advocacy

- Whenever you want to ask a question, make a conscious effort to supply the reasons for it, particularly if the other person is unlikely to know why you are asking it. Be alert to those situations where the other person looks puzzled or hesitates to reply. If this happens, supply your reason for asking the question.

  Review whether your inquiry resulted in your finding out what you really wanted to know.

Key exercise step 5:

Revising your words in terms of the open-to-learning model

Instructions for Step 5 of the key exercise are to be found in Appendix B under the heading **'Revising your words in terms of the open-to-learning model'** (page 250). This will guide you to write a new set of opening words for the difficult conversation you recorded in Step 1, in terms of the open-to-learning model.

8

Moving from Closed to Open Thinking in Difficult Conversations

---

Learning points

The factors that make our approach to a difficult conversation closed, are the same factors that make it very difficult to change from a closed to an open approach.

Being reflective practitioners helps us to make the transition from closed to open.

We can use the negative feelings that are associated with difficult conversations to 'alert' us to a problem and 'cue' us into making our thinking open.

The transition from a closed to an open approach to handling difficult conversations requires ongoing practice.

~~~~~~~~~~~~~~~~

Through a number of exercises, we invite you to practice using 'alert & cue' as a means of moving from a closed to an open way of operating.

As we explained in Chapter 1, this book addresses a serious problem. The closed and ineffective management of difficult conversations in the workplace is frequent and commonplace. It results in adverse outcomes: personal stress, poor working relationships, low morale and poor performance. We have argued that the reason why so many difficult conversations are handled ineffectively is because people's approach is typically based on a closed-to-learning model. In response to this problem, we have set out an open-to-learning conversational model. This model offers an effective way of managing difficult conversations and all of the beneficial outcomes this brings: decrease in stress, better working relationships, problems being directly addressed and jointly agreed, durable outcomes.

People behave in closed ways because of habitual and limited ways of thinking that operate swiftly and unconsciously. This can be a serious problem when we want to move from closed to open thinking, because we have to overcome the closed habits of a lifetime. In this chapter, we explore how we can overcome this problem so that we are able to operate in open mode throughout the course of any difficult conversation.

Making use of negative feelings: 'alert & cue'

Our experience is that it helps us to address the challenging task of moving from closed to open mode, if we first focus on any negative feelings that are raised by a difficult conversation. Negative feelings are a practically useful place to start because, as we indicated in Chapter 1, they are symptomatic of every difficult conversation. They are also relatively easy to identify.

Negative feelings (such as embarrassment, fearfulness, anger, frustration, resentment, guilt or confusion) can arise before a forthcoming conversation, during a conversation or after a conversation has finished.

Being aware of our negative feelings when they arise can 'alert' us to the fact that we are running into difficulties. By becoming alert in this way, we prevent ourselves from being driven, unthinkingly, into automatic, closed thinking. We can then use this awareness as a 'cue' to remember the principles and forms of words that make up the open model of conversation and to make the necessary changes from any thinking that is closed. We describe this strategy for moving from a closed to open approach as 'alert & cue'. We say more about this below.

Being a reflective practitioner

Practising being alert to our feelings and using these to cue us into 'thinking about our thinking' within the framework of the closed and open models, enables us to be reflective practitioners with regard to our difficult conversations. The term 'reflective practitioner' was coined by Schon (1983) and covers two useful processes; 'reflection-*on*-action' and 'reflection-*in*-action'.

Reflection-on-action

In relation to difficult conversations, reflection-on-action would apply to reflection before or after such a conversation. We can often be alerted to the need for reflection before a difficult conversation by the kind of negative feelings to which we have already referred above (see also Chapter 1, page 25). Such awareness can then cue us into preparing for that conversation with the three open-to-learning principles and the two open forms of words in mind.

Example
'I'm very worried... **alert**... that she won't listen to what I have to say... **cue**... Remember the principles of open conversation... I mustn't assume that this will be the case *(Principle One: Question any relevant assumptions).*'

In this example, noticing the negative feeling ('I'm very worried') acts as the alert, and this cues us into remembering Principle One of open-to-learning thinking.

We can also be alerted to the need to reflect on our handling of a difficult conversation that has gone badly by negative feelings that occur *after* such a conversation has finished

Example
'That conversation made me feel very angry with him... **alert**... **cue**... Remember the principles of open conversation... Perhaps I could have made the conversation into a partnership by finding out a bit more about his position *(Principle Two: Promote partnership).*'

Reflection-in-action

Reflection-on-action gives extremely useful practice in developing the skills of using our negative feelings to alert & cue us into using the open principles. However, what we really need to do is to become adept at using the open approach *whilst we are actually having* a difficult conversation. We need to become skilled at reflecting in action, so that we can achieve and maintain an open-to-learning approach throughout a difficult conversation

Here the use of alert & cue becomes an essential strategy for moving out of closed into open mode. The key to this transition is once again the negative feelings that difficult conversations inevitably produce. As soon as we become aware of such feelings *(alert)*, we need to use that awareness to make us think open and remember the principles of the open-to-learning model *(cue)*. This enables us, even during a very difficult conversation, to employ reflective skills. It enables us to become aware of our thinking and to review how one or more of the three principles of the open-to-learning model, and the forms of words that relate to these, might help us to handle the difficulties to which our feelings are alerting us.

Below we give two examples of how an alert & cue strategy might operate during a difficult conversation. (Many other examples of how this strategy might work are given in Chapter 9 where we explore how to deal with the ten types of difficult conversation from Chapter 5 in an open-to-learning way.)

Example
[taken from Conversation 1, Chapter 9 page 157]

Oh dear, I was afraid that this might come up. The real reason I haven't approved his promotion is that I've got concerns about his interpersonal skills... but I'm worried about saying that... there's no way he could cope with me telling him the real problem.

I'm worried...**alert**...
...**cue**... Remember the three principles.

I'm assuming he can't cope... but perhaps he could... I'm not sure *(Principle One: Question your assumptions)*... so I'll let him know there is a problem *(Principle Three: Promote the exchange of all relevant information)*... and let him decide whether he wants to know what the problem is *(Principle Two: Promote partnership).*'

Example
I'm really not doing very well in this conversation... and it's making me feel anxious.

I'm feeling anxious'...**alert**...
...**cue**...Remember the three principles.

I need to get back into partnership *(Principle Two: Promote partnership)*... I'll say I'm not happy with the way I'm handling the conversation *(Principle Three: Promote the exchange of all relevant information)* and ask if we can start again *(Principle Two: Promote partnership).*'

The need for ongoing, reflective practice

Being able to make the move from a closed approach, based on the habits of a lifetime, to an open way of handling difficult conversations requires, as with all other aspects of continuing professional development, constant reflective practice on our part. It is for this reason that we have provided the exercises that appear at the end of most of the chapters in the book. If you have tried out some of these, you will already have begun the process of learning to observe your own thinking. In so doing, you will have become more aware of how frequently one or all of the three characteristics of closed-to-learning thinking have informed and directed your thoughts, and how often the associated closed forms of words have resulted. You may also have tried out some of the exercises associated with an alternative conversational model – the open-to-learning model – and practised the three principles of open-to-learning thinking and the forms of words that give expression to them.

In this chapter we have added an important strategy, alert & cue, which you can practise to help you make the transition from a closed to an open mode of operating.

Learning to put the open-to-learning approach into practice takes time. Argyris (1992 pp. 33-34) notes, '...after the first few days of trying to learn quickly, most of our participants relaxed and slowed down. They realised that learning Model II[9] was going to be at least as difficult as learning to play, moderately well, a musical instrument or a sport.'

Practising an open approach to difficult conversations on a day-to-day basis, wherever and when ever you can, be that with family, friends or colleagues, in or outside of the working environment, will aid your own professional development in this area. If you can try out the open conversation approach in a group, alongside other learners, this will also be useful because it will enable you to learn from feedback and thus evaluate your thinking and words more accurately. So will undertaking training in how to use the open conversational model, through personal instruction and practice.[10]

The skill of reflection is essential if we are to gain conscious control over what we think and say during a difficult conversation. Only through being reflective practitioners will we be able to recognise how habitual is our closed thinking and be able to make the crucial switch to an open approach, in order to handle our difficult conversations effectively.

---

[9] Argyris' Model II corresponds to our open-to-learning model. See Appendix A for more information about Model II.
[10] See the Introduction for a link to information about the availability of such opportunities.

Exercises to help you move from closed to open thinking in your conversations

- Have a look at the annotated open conversations in Chapter 9 for examples of alert & cue being used to facilitate reflection-in-practice.

- Practise becoming aware of any negative feelings that you experience either before, during or after a conversation.

- When you find yourself anticipating a difficult conversation with negative feelings use these to *alert* you to a potential problem and to remind you *(cue)* of the three principles of open-to-learning thinking. Reflect on these in preparation for the forthcoming conversation.

- In order to make the association between *alert* and *cue* more spontaneous, rehearse the sequence: 'I'm feeling angry, upset, etc. ...**alert**...**cue**... Remember the principles of open conversation.' Such practice should help to make it easier to bring into play the three open-to-learning principles (and hence the forms of words that reflect these), whenever you become aware of negative feelings during a conversation.

- Look back on a conversation you have had, that has left you with negative feelings. (You may find the reminiscence exercise at the end of Chapter 1 helpful in recalling difficult conversations that you have already had, and their associated negative feelings). Use the framework of the closed and open-to-learning models to reflect on how you handled them.

9

Annotated Examples of the Open-to-Learning Approach

Learning points

How the switch from closed to open thinking during a conversation operates in practice.

How the open-to-learning approach plays out in ten difficult conversations.

How the open-to-learning approach results in beneficial outcomes for each of the ten conversations.

In Chapter 5, we looked at some annotated examples of closed-to-learning, ineffective approaches to ten types of difficult conversation. The conversations were between *A* (representing the person trying to manage the difficulty) and another person *B*. In this chapter we revisit these ten difficult conversations in order to illustrate the use of the open-to-learning model.

The ten types of difficult conversation

1. Saying something critical.
2. Communicating unwelcome information that we are obliged to convey.
3. Saying something you think will go against group consensus.
4. Retrieving a setback in an interpersonal relationship.
5. Engaging with someone who will not discuss things with us.
6. Dealing with a conflict of loyalties.
7. Coping with being criticised.

8. Responding to non-verbal behaviour that bothers us.
9. Responding to pressure to go beyond what we feel comfortable with.
10. Handling a conflict of views between ourselves and another person.

We show how the three principles (Chapter 6) and associated forms of words (Chapter 7) of the open-to-learning model enable *A* to manage the conversation effectively and bring about a number of beneficial outcomes. In particular we show how using the alert & cue strategy (Chapter 8) can help *A* make the transition from an initially closed to an open mode of operating.

These ten annotated conversations simply illustrate one possible open approach to a particular type of difficulty. For each difficulty there may be other ways of conducting the conversation in accordance with the open-to-learning model, all equally effective. The intention is that the examples will demonstrate the effectiveness of the open-to-learning model in addressing any kind of conversational difficulty.

How the annotated examples are set out

As in Chapter 5, the conversations are presented in two columns. *A*'s thoughts are on the left and *A*'s and *B*'s words on the right. *A*'s thoughts and words are numbered consecutively. In our analysis, we again focus on *A*, for the reasons given in Chapter 5 (page 79). To make it easier to relate to the script, *A*'s thoughts and words are repeated in the annotations, making use of the numbering already given.

As a reminder, we set out again the principles and forms of words typical of the open conversation model:

Thoughts:

Principle One:	Question any relevant assumptions.
Principle Two:	Promote partnership.
Principle Three:	Promote the exchange of all relevant information.

We have labelled *A*'s thoughts *assumptions* (indicating Principle One), *partnership* (indicating Principle Two) or *information* (indicating Principle Three), as appropriate, in order to draw attention to the particular principle that is shaping the thought concerned.

156

Forms of words:

Open advocacy:
- Advocacy is transparent.
- Advocacy with inquiry.

Open inquiry:
- Inquiry is genuine.
- Inquiry with advocacy.

1. Saying something critical (open approach)

A, a manager, is finding it difficult to tell *B* that the reason he (*B*) has not been promoted is because of his poor interpersonal skills.

How might *A* deal with her difficulty?

A's thoughts	*A* and *B*'s words
	B. I notice that over the last couple of years many of the people who've got the same sort of qualifications and experience as me are getting promotion or getting more responsibility. I'm not... and I'm wondering why that is... is there something the company's trying to tell me?
1) Oh dear, I was afraid this might come up, the real reason I haven't approved his promotion is that I've got concerns about his interpersonal skills... but I'm worried about saying that...there's no way he could cope with me telling him the real problem. I'm worried... **alert**... ...**cue**... Remember the principles of open conversation. (2) I'm assuming he can't cope but perhaps he could *(assumptions)*... I'm not sure... so, I'll let him know there is a problem *(information)*... and let him	

157

decide whether he wants to know what the problem is *(partnership)*.	
	A. (1) I think you're right to be concerned – I have considered promotion for you but, for a number of reasons, I have felt that hasn't been appropriate... I'm wondering whether you'd like me to tell you some of those reasons so that we can talk about them together?
	B. Well, yes, if there is some sort of reason for it then I'd certainly like to know what it is.
(3) That gives me the go-ahead to tell him what the problem is.... so I'll tell him *(information)*... and check whether he wants to hear more *(partnership)*.	
	A. (2) My main concern is to do with the way that you relate to other people. There have been occasions when you've got into quite serious arguments that have upset them. Would you like me to say a bit more about that?
	B. That's a bit of a shock to me... but yes, I suppose I need to hear more... please go ahead.

A's thoughts and words evaluated in terms of the components of the open-to-learning model

Thoughts (1)

'Oh dear, I was afraid this might come up, the real reason I haven't approved his promotion is that I've got concerns about his interpersonal skills... but I'm worried about saying that... there's no way he could cope with me telling him the real problem...

'I'm worried... **alert**...
...**cue**... Remember the principles of open conversation.'

Alert...cue. **A** identifies worried feelings *(alert)* and uses these to prompt her to think things through in terms of the three principles before replying

158

(cue), rather than letting herself be trapped into avoiding giving *B* the true reason for his lack of promotion.

Thoughts (2)

'I'm assuming he can't cope but perhaps he could *(assumptions)*... I'm not sure... so, I'll let him know there is a problem *(information)*... and let him decide whether he wants to know what the problem is *(partnership)*.'

Principle One (Question any relevant assumptions). By identifying her unquestioned assumption that *B* will not be able to cope with being told the real problem ('I'm assuming he can't cope'), and dealing with it by moderating what would otherwise be a certainty ('but perhaps he could'), *A* frees herself to be able to think in terms of the other two principles.

Principle Three (Promote the exchange of all relevant information). Informed by Principle Three, *A* decides to a give *B*'s question a direct reply ('so I'll let him know there's a problem').

Principle Two (Promote partnership in the conversation). Principle Two prompts *A* to offer *B* a choice in whether he wants further information ('and let him decide whether he wants to know what the problem is').

Words (1)

'I think you're right to be concerned – I have considered promotion for you but, for a number of reasons, I have felt that hasn't been appropriate... I'm wondering whether you'd like me to tell you some of those reasons so that we can talk about them together?'

Open advocacy (Advocacy is transparent). *A* makes explicit the fact that there is a problem ('I think you're right to be concerned.'). *A* also makes clear the origins of this statement ('I have felt...') and that she has some rationale for what she is saying ('for a number of reasons...') This is a powerful response from *A* because it is enables *B* to know that *A* is prepared to give him information that relates directly to his question about promotion.

Open inquiry (Inquiry with advocacy). *A* then invites *B* into further discussion of the issue ('and I'm wondering whether you'd like me to tell you some of those reasons'), making clear her reason for asking ('so that we can talk about them together'). By making her inquiry in this way *A* conveys to **B** that he has a genuine choice about whether to continue the conversation or not.

Thoughts (3)

'That gives me the go-ahead to tell him what the problem is... so I'll tell him *(information)*... and check whether he wants to hear more *(partnership)*.'

Principle Two (Promote partnership). **A** thinks again of acting in partnership with **B** ('check whether he wants to hear more'), rather than feeling obliged to think of making an independent, unilateral decision about what **B** can or cannot take.

Words (2)

'My main concern is to do with the way that you relate to other people. There have been occasions when you've got into quite serious arguments that have upset them. Would you like me to say a bit more about that?'

Open advocacy (Advocacy is transparent). **A** gives **B** more specific information about the problem ('My main concern is about the way that you relate to other people'). In this way **A** is able to let **B** know what the problem is and that **A** can substantiate the personal view that she has already given ('There have been occasions...').

Open advocacy (Advocacy with inquiry). **A** makes her advocacy even more open by coupling it with inquiry. She invites **B** to respond to what she has just said ('Would you like me to say a bit more about that?'). This further, genuine inquiry lets **B** know that he is still being treated as a partner in the conversation and that what happens next is still up to him.

Summary

By questioning her assumption that **B** will be unable to cope with the real reason for his lack of promotion, **A** has made it possible for herself to think of telling **B** what he wants to know. Her ongoing open-to-learning thoughts and forms of words make **B**'s concern – about his lack of promotion and the sensitive issue of his poor interpersonal skills – discussable. However unhappy **B** might be about the content of what is said, he is highly likely to feel that **A** has responded to his question directly and in a way that allowed him to be an equal partner in guiding the process of the conversation.

Outcomes

As a result of *A* working hard to make the real reason for *B*'s lack of promotion discussable, she brings about a number of beneficial outcomes.

For A. *A* can have a sense of competence as a manager, in that she has been able to say what she finds difficult to say (that the problem is *B*'s poor interpersonal skills) in a way that is likely to be acceptable to *B*.

For A and B's relationship. Although *B* may not like what he hears, the basis is established for a relationship in which difficult issues can be raised and discussed.

For the organisation. Since *B* now knows why he has not been promoted there is the possibility of him deciding to work on his interpersonal skills. Thus, he could become of more value to the organisation.

2. Communicating unwelcome information that we are obliged to convey (open approach)

A, a manager, has to tell *B*, a member of staff, that she is to be re-located. *A* is finding this difficult because he fears that *B* may be upset by the decision.

How might *A* deal with his difficulty?

A's thoughts	A and B's words
(1) I'm not looking forward to this. *B*'s going to be furious about the relocation decision – it'll mean further travelling for her and it may upset her child-care arrangements. I'm not looking forward to this ...**alert**... ...**cue**... Remember the principles of open conversation. (2) I'm assuming I know *B*'s reactions,	

but I really don't know exactly how this move is going to affect her – and I don't know how upset she's going to be *(assumptions)*.

Even if she doesn't like what I have to say, perhaps I can handle the meeting in a way that she will find acceptable.

At any rate, however upset she is, I'm obliged to tell her the decision... but I could also tell her who made it and why *(information)*... and find out how much she wants to know about the reasons for the decision *(partnership)*.

A. (1) *B*, I asked to see you because my senior manager has decided that we are going to have to lose one person from this office to the south area... and he has also decided that for a range of reasons you are the person with the skills that our south office could most easily use. You are therefore being transferred to the south office at the beginning of next month.

I'm aware that this has come up rather suddenly and you might like time to think about it... but I can tell you some more about the reasons for the decision, if you'd like me to?

B. I don't believe this. Why haven't I been consulted? And why me? Have you any idea how this move might affect my domestic arrangements! Why can't he transfer someone without children?

(3) OK – she is very upset. I will acknowledge her anger *(information)* and check how she wants to proceed *(partnership)*

A. (2) I can see that you're angry at the decision. ... and I'm wondering... do you want to go on talking about it now or would you like time to think about it first? As I say, I can give you more information about the reasons for the decision if you

	would like me to? **B**. You're right – I am angry... too angry to talk now. Once I've had a chance to calm down, I might feel like finding out more...

A's thoughts and words evaluated in terms of the components of the open-to-learning model

Thoughts (1)

'I'm not looking forward to this. **B**'s going to be furious about the re-location decision – it'll mean further travelling for her and it may upset her child-care arrangements.

'I'm not looking forward to this ...**alert**...
...**cue**... Remember the principles of open conversation.'

Alert...cue. Even before he makes his opening comments, *A* identifies feelings of anxiety *(alert)* and uses these to prompt him to think things through in terms of the three principles before replying *(cue)*, rather than letting himself be trapped into avoiding dealing with *B*'s possible reaction.

Thoughts (2)

'I'm assuming I know **B**'s reactions, but I really don't know exactly how this move is going to affect her – and I don't know how upset she's going to be *(assumptions)*. Even if she doesn't like what I have to say, perhaps I can handle the meeting in a way that she will find acceptable. At any rate, however upset she is, I'm obliged to tell her the decision... but I could tell her who made it and why *(information)*... and find out how much she wants to know about the reasons for the decision *(partnership)*.'

Principle One (Question any relevant assumptions). By identifying an unquestioned assumption ('I'm assuming I know *B*'s reactions'), and dealing with it by making it less certain ('I really don't know exactly how this move is going to affect her – and I don't know how upset she's going to be'), *A* frees himself from being driven into using closed-to-learning strategies. He is now able to focus on the Principles Two and Three to guide him into responding appropriately to whatever *B*'s reaction might be ('Even if she doesn't like what I have to say, perhaps I can handle the meeting in a way that she will find acceptable').

Principle Three (Promote the exchange of all relevant information). Principle Three prompts *A* to offer *B* information that will help B to understand something of the context and reason for the decision that has been made ('but I could also tell her who made it and why').

Principle Two (Promote partnership). Principle Two prompts *A* to involve *B* in deciding how to proceed by making it clear to *B* that she has a choice in deciding whether or not she wishes to hear more ('find out how much she wants to know').

Words (1)

'... I asked to see you because my senior manager has decided that we are going to have to lose one person from this office to the south area... and he has also decided that for a range of reasons you are the person with the skills that our south office could most easily use. You are therefore being transferred to the south office at the beginning of next month. I'm aware that this has come up rather suddenly and you might like time to think about it... but I can tell you some more about the reasons for the decision if you'd like me to?'

Open advocacy (Advocacy is transparent). A makes her information about *B*'s relocation transparent by giving *B* the rationale behind the decision.

Open advocacy (Advocacy with inquiry). A pairs advocacy ('I can tell you some more about the reasons for the decision...') with a question to check if this is what *B* wants ('... if you'd like me to?'). In doing so, *A* makes it possible for *B* to be involved in the management of the conversation.

Thoughts (3)

'OK – she is very upset. I will acknowledge her anger *(information)* and check how she wants to proceed *(partnership).*'

Principle Three (Promote the exchange of all relevant information). Principle Three prompts *A* to check *B*'s wishes again ('and check how she wants to proceed').

Principle Two (Promote partnership). This principle prompts *A* to acknowledge *B*'s anger and to check *B*'s wishes again ('and check how she wants to proceed').

Words (2)

'I can see that you're angry at the decision... and I'm wondering... do you want to go on talking about it now or would you like time to think about it first? As I say, I can give you more information about the reasons for the decision if you would like me to?'

Open advocacy (Advocacy with inquiry). A follows up his words, 'I can see that you're angry at the decision', with an inquiry that offers *B* a choice as to how *B* wants to proceed ('do you want to go on talking about it now or...?'). In doing so, *A* indicates that he has registered *B*'s feelings and sees that they need to be addressed.

Open advocacy (Advocacy with inquiry). A also invites *B* to respond to his offer of further information ('As I say, I can give you more information about the reasons for the decision if you would like me to?'). Thus *B* is left in no doubt that, within the context of a decision that has already been made, *A* is prepared to continue to discuss the situation in a way that allows *B* to be involved in the management of the conversation.

Summary

By questioning his assumption that he can predict *B*'s reactions *A* is able to focus on making the news of *B*'s relocation and, especially her reaction to it, discussable. Although *B* may not like what she is told, she is likely to feel that, within the constraints of the situation, *A* has managed to say what he had to say and, at the same time, has respected the fact that *B* has strong feelings, thus helping to maintain the working relationship.

Outcomes

Given that *A* is obliged to communicate news that is unwelcome to *B*, and because he has worked hard at making the issues as discussable as possible, the conversation is likely to have a number of beneficial outcomes.

For A. A can feel that he has acted in a professionally competent manner in fulfilling his obligation to give unwelcome information to *B* while still keeping open the possibility of further discussion with *B*.

For A and B's relationship. B may very well not have liked the information in the conversation that *A* gave her. However she would probably acknowledge that the way that *A* gave her the information and offered her choices was as helpful as was within *A*'s power. To that extent their working relationship is not likely ultimately to be damaged.

For the organisation. As a result of *A*'s professionalism there is a possibility that *B* may be able to bring herself to hear the reasons for her relocation and, if those reasons are acceptable to her, to reconcile herself to the decision – to the benefit of the organisation – rather than becoming disaffected.

3. Saying something we think will go against group consensus (open approach)

A, a section manager, is attending one of his monthly meetings with a group of other section managers, *B* being the chairperson. *A* increasingly feels that the meetings take up a lot of his time and that they are not particularly productive. However, he is worried that if he brings this up he may provoke hostility from in his colleagues.

How might *A* deal with his difficulty?

A's thoughts	*A* and *B*'s words
	B. Has anyone got any issues they'd like to raise under AOB?
(1) I'm so fed up with these meetings – they take up the whole afternoon... whether there's anything important to discuss or not... nothing particularly useful comes out of them for me...	
I'd really like to tell the others, but I'm worried that if I say anything negative about the meetings... which they seem to enjoy... I'm bound to get their backs up... and then they'll close ranks on me and make me feel even worse...	
I'm worried ...**alert**... ...**cue**... Remember the principles of open conversation.	
(2) I'm assuming how the others will react but it may be possible for me to	

say what's on my mind in such a way that it won't get people's backs up *(assumptions)*. I could simply present it as a problem I'm having *(information)*... and ask them to talk it over with me *(partnership)*.	
	A. (1) Yes. I've got a problem. I'm finding it hard to justify the time I spend attending these meetings. They take up the whole afternoon whether or not, from my perspective, there's anything important to discuss... ... I'd welcome a discussion about this if people are willing?

A's thoughts and words evaluated in terms of the components of the open-to-learning model

Thoughts (1)

'I'm so fed up with these meetings – they take up the whole afternoon... whether there's anything important to discuss or not... nothing particularly useful comes out of them for me...I'd really like to tell the others, but I'm worried that if I say anything negative about the meetings... which they seem to enjoy... I'm bound to get their backs up... and then they'll close ranks on me and make me feel even worse.

'I'm worried ...**alert**...
...**cue**... Remember the principles of open conversation.'

Alert...cue. A is able to identify negative feelings of worry *(alert)* and use these to prompt him to think things through in terms of the three principles *(cue)*, rather than letting himself be trapped by his closed thinking into saying nothing.

Thoughts (2)

'I'm assuming how the others will react but it may be possible for me to say what's on my mind in such a way that it won't get people's

167

backs up *(assumptions)*. I could simply present it as a problem I'm having *(information)*... and ask them to talk it over with me *(partnership)*.'

Principle One (Question any relevant assumptions). A identifies his unquestioned assumption ('I'm assuming how the others will react') and deals with it by reframing it as: '... it may be possible for me to say what's on my mind in such a way that it won't get people's backs up...'. In so doing, A stops himself from being driven to stay silent by his worries. He is now free to use the other two principles to guide him as to how he might safely raise the issue.

Principle Three (Promote the exchange of relevant information). Principle Three prompts A to remember to make the 'origins/ownership' of the problem clear – that it is *his* problem ('I could simply present it as a problem I'm having'), rather than there being something inherently wrong with the meeting.

Principle Two (Promote partnership). Principle Two prompts A to think in terms of inviting his colleagues to make his problem the subject of general discussion ('and ask them to talk it over with me').

Words (1)

'Yes. I've got a problem. I'm finding it hard to justify the time I spend attending these meetings. They take up the whole afternoon whether or not, from my perspective, there's anything important to discuss... I'd welcome a discussion about this if people are willing?'

Open advocacy (Advocacy is transparent). A states explicitly that there is a problem. His advocacy provides enough information for colleagues to be able to evaluate the status of that problem. A's advocacy covers the nature of the difficulty and that it is his problem and his perspective. Because A owns the problem as his, his colleagues are unlikely to feel that A is blaming them. They are therefore unlikely to react negatively to A's words.

Open advocacy (Advocacy with inquiry). A pursues his open advocacy by following it with an inquiry that invites others into a discussion of his problem ('I'd welcome a discussion about my difficulty if people are willing?'). A's invitation to a discussion puts his colleagues in the position of being asked to help A to solve A's problem. It conveys A's wish to find a solution that will be acceptable to all.

168

Summary

A questions his assumption that his colleagues will close ranks against him if he communicates his concerns about the meetings. This allows him to focus on making his difficulty discussable. As a result he maximises the likelihood that his concern can be addressed without damage to his working relationship with the rest of the group.

Outcomes

As a result of working hard at making the issues discussable the conversation is likely to have a number of beneficial outcomes.

For A. Whatever his colleague's response, *A* can feel satisfied that he has been able to raise his concern at an appropriate moment.

For A and B's relationship. With *A*'s concern 'on the table', *A*'s relationship with his colleagues in future meetings will be based on his real views rather than possibly being undermined by undisclosed resentment on *A*'s part.

For the organisation. *A* has aired a potential organisational problem, and has opened up the possibility of it being dealt with in a way in which all those who attend the meetings can be involved.

4. Retrieving a setback in an interpersonal relationship (open approach)

A, a manager knows that *B*, a member of her staff, is angry with her, because she was abrupt with *B* in a recent conversation. *A* wants to restore a positive working relationship with *B* but she is anxious that in doing this she will lose credibility as a manager.

How might *A* deal with her difficulty?

A's thoughts	*A* and *B*'s words
(1) I know that *B*'s angry with me because I snapped at her this	

morning... I shouldn't have done that... but on the other hand **B** should have known better than to choose a moment when I was busy to give me her views.

I'd like to put things right but I'm feeling quite uncomfortable because it doesn't look good for a manager to apologise or admit blame...

I'm feeling uncomfortable... **alert**... ...**cue**... Remember the principles of open conversation.

(2) Check my assumptions! Even though I'm her manager perhaps there's a way that I can still talk to her person to person without losing my authority *(assumptions)*...

I'll refer to what happened, make clear that I feel bad because I was partly responsible *(information)* and see if she's willing to talk about it *(partnership)*.

A. (1) **B**, this morning I needed to give all my attention to what I was doing, and I know that I was abrupt with you when you tried to get my attention.

I feel bad about that and I'd like to talk about what happened. Can we do that?

B. Well I was pretty angry when it happened... I still am as a matter of fact... but I'd rather talk it through than let it stay simmering.

A's thoughts and words evaluated in terms of the components of the open-to-learning model

Thoughts (1)

'I know that *B*'s angry with me because I snapped at her this morning... I shouldn't have done that... but on the other hand *B* should have known better than to choose a moment when I was busy to give me her views. I'd like to put things right but I'm feeling quite uncomfortable because it doesn't look good for a manager to apologise or admit blame...

'I'm feeling uncomfortable... **alert**...
...**cue**... Remember the principles of open conversation.'

Alert...cue. Even before *A* approaches *B*, she has identified negative feelings *(alert)* and used these to prompt her to think through her approach to *B* in terms of the three principles *(cue)*. This prevents her being trapped into trying to conform to her idea of what a manager 'should' do.

Thoughts (2)

'Check my assumptions! Even though I'm her manager perhaps there's a way that I can still talk to her person to person without losing my authority *(assumptions)*... I'll refer to what happened, make clear that I feel bad because I was partly responsible *(information)* and see if she's willing to talk about it *(partnership)*.'

Principle One (Question any relevant assumptions). *A* deals with her previously unquestioned assumption that it doesn't look good for managers to apologise or admit blame, by trying to see her managerial authority differently ('even though I'm her manager I can still talk to her person to person without losing my authority'). In so doing, *A* frees herself to be able to think through her approach to *B* in terms of the other two principles.

Principle Three (Promote the exchange of all relevant information). *A* decides to raise explicitly the issue which tacitly lies between them – that *B* is angry with her for snapping at her earlier in the day. *A* also plans to let *B* know how things look from her point of view and how she feels about the situation ('I'll refer to what happened, make clear that I feel bad because I was partly responsible').

Principle Two (Promote partnership). Because *A* wants to restore the relationship but is not sure about *B*'s position, she decides to invite *B* into a

171

discussion about what happened ('and see if she's willing to talk about it').

Words (1)

'*B*, this morning I needed to give all my attention to what I was doing, and I know that I was abrupt with you when you tried to get my attention. I feel bad about that and I'd like to talk about what happened. Can we do that?'

Open advocacy (Advocacy is transparent). *A*'s advocacy contains enough information to let *B* know what is troubling her ('*B*... I know that I was abrupt with you when you tried to get my attention'), and how she feels about it ('I feel bad about that'). Because she lets *B* know how she is feeling and why, and because she makes it clear that it is her (*A*'s) problem, *A*'s words are likely to come over as direct and non-reproachful.

Open advocacy (Advocacy with inquiry). *A* suggests a way forward ('and I'd like to talk about what happened') and pairs this with a question that invites *B* into such a discussion ('Can we do that?'). *A*'s suggestion and invitation enables *B* to see that *A* is giving her the opportunity (should she want to take it) to offer her own interpretation of what happened and that *A* is serious about putting things right between them.

Summary

A questions her assumption about what is and is not appropriate for a manager to do. This frees her to use the skills of open conversation to make her abruptness of the morning discussable.

Outcomes

By making the events of the morning discussable *A* has brought about a number of beneficial outcomes.

For A. *A* can feel satisfied that she has handled the conversation with *B* in a way that is consistent with her responsibilities as a manager.

For A and B's relationship. There is a good chance that the issue between *A* and *B* will be sorted out so that they can continue to work together without underlying tension.

For the organisation. The organisation is likely to benefit from a renewed working relationship between *A* and *B*.

5. Responding to someone who will not discuss things with us (open approach)

A, a hard pressed administrative assistant, is, once again, given even more work that is urgent by her senior manager *B*. On past experience *A* believes it will be pointless to say 'no', as *B* does not take her problem seriously.

How might *A* deal with her difficulty?

A's thoughts	*A* and *B*'s words
	B. *A*, I need the Departmental Progress Report completed urgently – the meeting's been brought forward to tomorrow.
(1) Oh no!... I'm already up to here with his urgent work... I'll tell him that it's impossible... but I'm feeling really stressed because he never listens to me.	
I'm feeling stressed... **alert**... ...**cue**... Remember the principles of open conversation.	
(2) Perhaps he will listen to me *(assumptions)* if this time I tell him my position *(information)* and ask if we can talk about it *(partnership)*, so that he sees that I'm really serious.	
	A. (1) Look, I really can't take any more on – I'm fully stretched as it is... can we talk about this?
	B. I know. We're all under pressure... but this really is urgent... I'm sure I can rely on you to find a way of fitting it in.
(3) He's not hearing me... let's try asking again *(partnership)*.	
	A. (2) No. I genuinely can't fit this in with all your other work and I really would like to talk to you about it.
	B. Look, *A*, you know what you've got to

	do – just fit it in the best way you can.
(4) He's still not hearing me… I think I've got to let him know that it's not just my problem… it affects him as well, because some of the work just won't get done *(information)*… I'll give him a choice as to who decides *(partnership)*.	
	A. (3) If I do this it means that I will have to leave some of your other urgent work. Now I'm quite happy to decide myself which bits of your work I leave, but you may prefer to be the one who decides?
	B. Ah… well… if something has got to be postponed I suppose I need to work out the priorities. Can you give me a list of what you have to do?

A's thoughts and words evaluated in terms of the components of the open-to-learning model

Thoughts (1)

'Oh no!… I'm already up to here with his urgent work… I'll tell him that it's impossible… but I'm feeling really stressed because he never listens to me.

'I'm feeling stressed… **alert**…
…**cue**… Remember the principles of open conversation.'

Alert…cue. Before she makes her first response, *A* identifies negative feelings of stress *(alert)* and uses these to prompt her to think things through in terms of the three principles before responding to *B* *(cue)*. She thus avoids being trapped by her previous pattern of behaviour and giving in to him against her own wishes.

Thoughts (2)

'Perhaps he will listen to me *(assumptions)* if this time I tell him my position *(information)* and ask if we can talk about it *(partnership)*, so that he sees that I'm really serious.'

Principle One (Question any relevant assumptions). **A** deals with her unquestioned assumption that **B** 'never listens' by thinking of this assumption as a possibility rather than a certainty ('Perhaps he will listen to me if I ask if we can talk about'). This frees her to give attention to how she replies to **B** using Principles Two and Three.

Principle Two (Promote partnership). Principle Two prompts **A** to try to involve **B** in solving the problem ('and ask if we can talk about it').

Principle Three (Promote the exchange of all relevant information). Principle Three prompts **A** to make sure **B** knows her position.

Words (1)

> 'Look, I really can't take any more on – I'm fully stretched as it is... can we talk about this?'

Open advocacy (Advocacy with inquiry). **A** not only makes her problem of being overstretched clear to **B** ('I really can't take any more on – I'm fully stretched as it is'), she also requests a discussion ('can we talk about this?'). In doing this she makes it a little harder for **B** to ignore her problem.

Thoughts (3)

> 'He's not hearing me... let's try asking again *(partnership)*.'

Principle Two (Promote partnership). **A** notes that **B** is still ignoring her problem ('he's not hearing me') but does not allow this to stop her from persisting in her request for a discussion.

Words (2)

> 'No. I genuinely can't fit this in with all your other work and I really would like to talk to you about it.'

Open advocacy (Advocacy with inquiry). **A** repeats her statement that she is overloaded and pairs this with a request to talk about it. She thus gives **B** a second opportunity to discuss the problem with her.

Thoughts (4)

> 'He's still not hearing me... I think I've got to let him know that it's not just my problem... it affects him as well, because some of the work just won't get done *(information)*... I'll give him a choice as to who decides *(partnership)*.'

Principle Three (Promote the exchange of all relevant information). Since **B** has twice ignored **A**'s request for further discussion, **A** realises that the information she has given **B** is not enough to convince **B** that the issue is sufficiently serious for him to discuss it with her. She is thus prompted to ensure that **B** is fully in the picture. This means letting **B** know the possible consequences for him (**B**) – that her (**A**'s) problem will become a problem for **B** too if he continues to refuse to become involved in helping her deal with it.

Principle Two (Promote partnership). **A** plans to offer **B** a choice as to what work will or will not be done, in the hope of promoting a partnership in which **B** takes the issue seriously.

Words (3)

'If I do this it means that I will have to leave some of your other work. Now I'm quite happy to decide myself which bits of your work I leave, but you may prefer to be the one who decides?'

Open advocacy (Advocacy is transparent). In the face of **B**'s lack of concern, **A** increases the force of her advocacy by including further information that is directly relevant to **B** ('If I do this it means that I will have to leave some of your other urgent work. Now I'm quite happy to decide myself which bits of your work I leave'). The information about what the consequences for **B** will be if he fails to become involved is probably the best that **A** can do to get **B** to take what she says seriously. **A**'s words do not guarantee that **B** will take up her suggestion that he prioritises the work. However, they do oblige **B** to see that this is not purely **A**'s problem but one that he needs to share with her.

Open advocacy (Advocacy with inquiry). **A** makes it clear that she is prepared to make the decision about which work to leave ('I'm quite happy to decide') and so her question ('but you may prefer to be the one who decides?') offers **B** a genuine choice – help to prioritise the work, or risk that the work he considers a priority will be left undone.

Summary

A questions her assumption that it is fruitless to try to get her manager to listen to her. This frees her to use her skills in open conversation to make her problem discussable. Although her manager may not wish to be drawn into a discussion, he is nevertheless likely to see the sense of doing so because of the likely adverse consequences for him if he does not.

Outcomes

By working hard to make her problem about accepting more work discussable, *A* has brought about some beneficial outcomes.

For A. *A* is likely to end up with a more manageable workload. She can also feel that she has managed to get *B* to take notice of her concerns. This is likely to enhance her self-esteem.

For A and B's relationship. *A* has learnt that she can get *B* to engage with her concerns in a way that maintains good working relationships and is likely to feel more able to have her views taken seriously by *B* in future discussions.

For the organisation. The organisation will benefit from a prioritisation of *A*'s work that allows her to produce it to her usual standard and on time.

6. Dealing with a conflict of loyalties (open approach)

A, a manager, is approached by a member of staff, *B*, with a complaint that *B*'s colleague *X*, is not pulling her weight and that *B* wishes to work with someone else. *A* is sympathetic to *B*'s situation but has been told, in confidence, that *X* is on medication that affects her concentration and should be protected from any changes that might add to her problems. *A* feels a conflict of loyalties between his sympathy for *B* and his wish to protect *X*.

How might *A* deal with his difficulty?

A's thoughts	*A* and *B*'s words
(1) I'm torn between the two of them! I can see *B*'s problem but *X* needs stability… and I can't tell *B* about *X*'s	*B.* *A*, I'm not at all happy to go on working with *X*. She's not been pulling her weight recently and I'm constantly having to cover for her. Do you think you could arrange for me to work with someone else?

177

difficulty without breaking **X**'s confidence... I think I'd better just say no firmly, but also give **B** a positive stroke or two and hope for the best...

I'm torn between the two of them!...
alert...
...**cue**... Remember the principles of open conversation.

(2) I'm assuming that I've got to choose between moving one of them – but I can't do this as it will mean changing **X**'s situation, which I've been told I shouldn't do... and hoping that **B** will stick with the situation if he knows about the medication – but this would mean breaking **X**'s confidence, which I don't want to do either...

... but maybe I don't have to make that choice... there may be ways of dealing with **B**'s difficulty that keep him as **X**'s partner without breaking **X**'s confidence *(assumptions)*.

But first I need to let him know that though I acknowledge his problem I can't move either of them *(information)*... and check that he understands that for reasons of confidentiality I can only give him a limited explanation *(partnership)*.

A. (1) I've noticed that you have been taking on some of **X**'s work recently and I think we need to sort that out. However, I'm afraid I can't move either of you elsewhere at this point... I have good reasons for this that I wish I could tell you. But at the moment I'm not in a position to do so without breaking confidence. Can you accept that I'm in a bit of a dilemma?

B. Well, I suppose I'll have to, but it still leaves me with my problem.

(3) He's absolutely right and he needs to know that I take it seriously *(information)*. I wonder if he would be prepared to discuss ways of improving his situation without moving either of them? *(partnership)*	**A.** (2) Yes, I agree... and since I don't feel able to move either of you at the moment, how about us giving some thought to other ways of making your job more manageable? **B.** Well... if you can think of anything... yes... it's not as though I've got anything personal against **X**. But something's got to be done...

A's thoughts and words, evaluated in terms of the components of the open-to-learning model

Thoughts (1)

'I'm torn between the two of them! I can see **B**'s problem but **X** needs stability... and I can't tell **B** about **X**'s difficulty without breaking **X**'s confidence... I think I'd better just say no firmly, but also give **B** a positive stroke or two and hope for the best...

'I'm torn!... **alert**...

...**cue**... Remember the principles of open conversation.'

Alert...cue. Before making a response to **B**'s request, *A* identifies negative feelings of conflict, 'I'm torn' *(alert)*, and he uses these to prompt himself to think things through in terms of the three principles before replying *(cue)*, rather than let himself be trapped into having to choose between loyalty to **B** or loyalty to **X**.

Thoughts (2)

'I'm assuming that I've got to choose between moving one of them – but I can't do this as it will mean changing **X**'s situation, which I've been told I shouldn't do... and hoping that **B** will stick with the situation if he knows about the medication – but this would mean breaking **X**'s confidence, which I don't want to do either... but maybe I don't have to make that choice... there may be ways of dealing with B's difficulty that keep him as **X**'s partner without breaking **X**'s

179

confidence *(assumptions)*. But first I need to let him know that though I acknowledge his problem I can't move either of them *(information)...* and check that he understands that for reasons of confidentiality I can only give him a limited explanation *(partnership).*'

Principle One (Question any relevant assumptions). A identifies and deals with his assumption that he has to choose between loyalty to either *B* or *X* by trying to imagine an alternative way of seeing things. This releases him from his dilemma and allows him to focus on the difficulty before him – *B*'s problem with his work situation. *A* is now free to use the other two principles in finding a way forward that is acceptable to both parties.

Principle Three (Promote the exchange of all relevant information). Principle Three prompts *A* to let *B* know that *B*'s solution to the problem – working with someone else – is not one *A* can agree to ('I can't move either of them') and to explain that he is not in a position to disclose confidential information ('for reasons of confidentiality...').

Principle Two (Promote partnership). Principle Two prompts *A* to involve *B* in the conversation by explicitly acknowledging his problem and by checking that *B* understands his difficulty with confidentiality.

Words (1)

'I've noticed that you have been taking on some of *X*'s work recently and I think we need to sort that out. However I'm afraid I can't move either of you at this point. I have good reasons for this that I wish I could tell you; but at the moment I'm not in a position to do so without breaking confidence. Can you accept that I'm in a bit of a dilemma?'

Open advocacy (Advocacy is transparent). A lets *B* know that he has heard what *B* is saying by acknowledging his problem ('I've noticed... we need to sort that out'). *A*'s advocacy also includes as much information as he is able to give ('I do have good reasons for this'), including the reason why he is unable to give him more ('at the moment I'm not in a position to do so without breaking confidence'). *A*'s words let *B* know that his problem has been heard and that *A* has done his best, within the constraints of the situation, to explain why he is not able to go along with *B*'s request.

Open advocacy (Advocacy with inquiry). A makes his advocacy even more open by checking that *B* is willing to accept that he has a problem in doing what *B* asks ('Can you accept that I'm in a bit of a dilemma?'). *A*'s inquiry is intended to communicate to *B* that his views count in the discussion.

180

Thoughts (3)

'He's absolutely right and he needs to know that I take it seriously *(information)*. I wonder if he would be up for discussing ways of improving his situation without moving either of them *(partnership)*?'

Principle Three (Promote the exchange of all relevant information). **A** decides to make sure that **B** knows that he takes his problem seriously.

Principle Two (Promote partnership). **A** thinks in terms of inviting **B** to solve his problem in partnership with him (I wonder if he would be up for discussing...').

Words (2)

'Yes, I agree... and since I don't feel able to move either of you at the moment how about us giving some thought to other ways of making your job more manageable?'

Open inquiry (Inquiry with advocacy). **A** invites **B** to join him in considering alternative solutions to **B**'s problem ('How about us giving some thought to other ways of making your job more manageable?'), and explains why he is making this suggestion ('since I don't feel able to move either of you'). These words are intended to let **B** know that **A** is concerned about his situation and make it clear why **A** is inviting him to consider an alternative way forward.

Summary

By questioning his assumption that he has to choose between the needs of **B** and **X**, **A** enables himself to focus on finding a way forward that meets the needs of both of them. His open-to-learning thoughts and forms of words make the problematic situation discussable. In addition the offer of further discussion about how to make **B**'s job more manageable is likely to be helpful to **B**.

Outcomes

By taking **B**'s problem seriously and making it discussable, **A** has brought about the following beneficial outcomes.

For A. **A** can feel satisfied that there is a possibility of coming up with a way forward to the work situation that is manageable for both **B** and **X**, and that he has brought this about without breaking any confidentiality.

For A and B's relationship. Even though he is under some constraint, *A*'s willingness to take *B*'s problem seriously and to involve *B* in that process is very likely to promote a positive working relationship.

For the organisation. There is a strong likelihood that the problem of the current imbalance and inefficiency in *B* and *X*'s working relationship can eventually be dealt with.

7. Coping with being criticised (open approach)

A finds it difficult to cope with *B*, a fellow manager, telling him that he (*B*) did not like the way *A* chaired the management meeting.

How might *A* handle his difficulty?

A's thoughts	A and B's words
	B. You know, *A*, I really didn't like the way you chaired the meeting just now.
(1) I really find that annoying – I ran the meeting well…	
I'm annoyed… **alert**… …**cue**… Remember the principles of open conversation.	
(2) I'm pretty sure I ran things well, but perhaps *B* has picked up on something that could be improved *(assumptions)*… let's find out *(information)*… and make sure he realises that I really want to know *(partnership)*.	*A*. (1) Hmmm…I'd be interested to know what it was that makes you feel that way? There's always room for improvement.
	B. Oh… well, I felt that you didn't manage the agenda very well. You gave so much time to the early items that we

	had to rush the last few – even though they were equally important.
(3) I thought I controlled the exchange of views well for each agenda item... but it is difficult to anticipate the time that each item will take *(assumptions)*... I'll let **B** know that he's given me something to think about *(information)/(partnership)*.	
	A. (2) You may have a point there... I'll think about what you say.

A's thoughts and words evaluated in terms of the components of the open-to-learning model

Thoughts (1)

'I really find that annoying – I ran the meeting well.

'I'm annoyed... **alert**...

...**cue**... Remember the principles of open conversation.'

Alert ...cue. **A** identifies feelings of annoyance *(alert)* and uses these to prompt him to think things through in terms of the three principles before replying *(cue)*. He thus avoids being trapped in a defensive position.

Thoughts (2)

'I'm pretty sure I ran things well, but perhaps **B** has picked up on something that could be improved *(assumptions)*... let's find out *(information)*... and make sure he realises that I really want to know *(partnership)*.'

Principle One (Question any relevant assumptions). **A** deals with his assumption that he ran the meeting well by making it a little less certain ('I'm pretty sure I ran things well') and by recognising that this does not exclude other possible ways of seeing things ('perhaps **B** has picked up on something that could be improved'). In doing this, **A** makes himself open-to-learning. Rather than seeing **B**'s views as something to be dismissed out of hand or threatening, **A** is now able to listen to **B** and consider what he says on its merits.

Principle Three (Promote the exchange of all relevant information). This principle prompts *A* to find out what it is that *B* has picked up ('let's find out') and to offer *B* the reason for his request so that *B* realises that the request is genuine ('and make sure he realises that I really want to know').

Words (1)

'Hmmm... I'd be interested to know what it was that makes you feel that way? There's always room for improvement.'

Open inquiry (Inquiry with advocacy). In pairing his question ('I'd be interested to know what it was that makes you feel that way?') with advocacy ('There's always room for improvement') *A* makes the reason for his inquiry clear. Linking inquiry with advocacy in this way is powerful because it is likely to reduce any doubts that *B* may have about the reasons for *A*'s inquiry. For example, without *A*'s advocacy, *B* might otherwise wonder if *A*'s question is some form of put-down, rather than an acknowledgement of what *B* has said.

Thoughts (3)

'I thought I controlled the exchange of views well for each agenda item... but it is difficult to anticipate the time that each item will take *(assumptions)*... I'll let *B* know that he's given me something to think about *(information)/(partnership)*.'

Principle One (Question any relevant assumptions). *A* continues to question his own assumption that he chaired the meeting well. Consequently he is able to hear and evaluate *B*'s comments on their merits.

Principles Three (Promote the exchange of all relevant information) and Two (Promote partnership). These principles prompt *A* to let *B* know that he intends to take *B*'s views seriously and, at the same time, that he sees *B*'s comments as a basis for partnership rather than for adversarial rivalry.

Words (2)

'You may have a point there... I'll think about what you say.'

Open advocacy (Advocacy is transparent). *A* openly acknowledges the potential usefulness of *B*'s observations. His words ('I'll think about what you say') are likely to convey to *B* that his comments are being taken seriously and give encouraging feedback to *B*.

Summary

By questioning his assumption that he ran the meeting well (and therefore has nothing to learn from **B**) **A** is able to make **B**'s initially disturbing comments discussable. It also enables him to treat **B**'s comment on its merits.

Outcomes

By his constructive handling of **B**'s comment **A** achieves a number of beneficial outcomes.

For A. **A** has put himself in a position where he is prepared to consider **B**'s views on how he might improve the way he chairs meetings.

For A and B's relationship. **A** is likely to comes over as open to learning rather than defensive or dismissive. This is highly likely to foster a working relationship that acknowledges and accommodates alternative views.

For the organisation. The organisation will benefit if **A** is willing to review and, if necessary, change the way he chairs meetings. Cooperative interactions between two of its managers will also benefit the organisation.

8. Responding to non-verbal behaviour that bothers us (open approach)

A, a trainee manager, is presenting his section plan to **B**, his line manager, when he notices **B** frowning. This raises his anxieties.

How might **A** deal with his anxiety?

A's thoughts	**A** and **B**'s words
	(**B** frowns as **A** is presenting his section plan)
(1) **B**'s frowning... that means he doesn't like my plan... that's a bit discouraging... I don't think he realises how well researched it is... I'd better explain that what I'm giving him at the moment is only a summary ...	

I'm feeling a bit discouraged... **alert**... ...**cue**... Remember the principles of open conversation. (2) I could be making a wrong assumption here. *B*'s frown may not mean what I think *(assumptions)*... I'd better find out before I go on...*(information)*.	
	A. (1) I noticed you frowning just now... I'm wondering if you're not happy about what I'm saying...?
	B. No, I'm very happy with what you're saying – I didn't realise I was frowning... I was actually considering the implications of what you're saying for the business plan...
(3) So that's what the frown was about... if *B*'s generally happy with what I'm saying I wonder if it might be a good idea for us to give some thought to its implications for the business plan ... let's check how *B* feels about that *(partnership)*.	
	A. (2) Oh right. Should we use the time to look at the implications for the business plan, or should I carry on with explaining my plans? Which would you prefer?
	B. Actually, I think it would be useful to spend some time exploring the implications first...

A's thoughts and words evaluated in terms of the components of the open-to-learning model

Thoughts (1)

'B's frowning... that means he doesn't like my plan... that's a bit discouraging...I don't think he realises how well researched it is... I'd better explain that what I'm giving him at the moment is only a summary...

'I'm feeling a bit discouraged... **alert**...
...**cue**... Remember the principles of open conversation.'

Alert...cue. *B*'s frown initially provokes a negative reaction from *A*. He makes the assumption that *B* does not like his plan and goes so far as to contemplate a closed-to-learning response. However *A* takes note of his feelings of discouragement *(alert)* and allows these to cue him in to thinking in terms of the three principles *(cue)*. This prevents him from being trapped in a defensive position by his otherwise unchecked assumptions.

Thoughts (2)

'I could be making a wrong assumption here. *B*'s frown may not mean what I think *(assumptions)*... I'd better find out before I go on *(information)*...'

Principle One (Question any relevant assumptions). *A* deals with his assumption – that *B*'s frown means *B* doesn't like his plan – by questioning it ('I could be making a wrong assumption here. *B*'s frown may not mean what I think'), and by deciding to check it out with *B* ('I'd better find out before I go on...').

Principle Three (Promote the exchange of all relevant information). *A* decides to mention *B*'s non-verbal behaviour (his frown) explicitly rather than treat it as a no-go area for discussion.

Words (1)

'I noticed you frowning just now... I'm wondering if you're not happy about what I'm saying...?'

Open advocacy (Advocacy is transparent). *A* gives specific information ('I noticed you frowning')...

Open advocacy (advocacy with inquiry)... before making his inquiry ('I'm wondering if you're not happy about what I'm saying...?') in order to explain why he is asking the question. Had *A* not mentioned *B*'s frown, his checking out question ('I'm wondering....?') might have puzzled or worried *B*.

Thoughts (3)

'So that's what the frown was about... if *B*'s generally happy with what I'm saying I wonder if it might be a good idea for us to give some thought to its implications for the business plan... let's check how *B* feels about that *(partnership)*.'

Principle Two (Promote partnership). The new information that *A*'s checking out has elicited (*B*'s words: 'I was actually considering the implications of what you're saying for the business plan...') has removed *A*'s concerns ('So that's what the frown was about'). This now enables *A* to think in terms of involving *B* in the conduct of the meeting by offering him the option of an alternative direction ('I wonder if it might be a good idea for us to give some thought to its implications for the business plan... let's check how *B* feels about that...').

Words (2)

'Oh right. Should we use the time to look at the implications for the business plan, or should I carry on with explaining my plans? Which would you prefer?'

Open advocacy (Advocacy with inquiry). *A* conveys that he has heard *B* by incorporating *B*'s response into his statement ('Should we use the time to look at the implications for the business plan, or should I carry on with explaining my plans?'). He pairs this with an invitation to *B* to share in the decision-making ('Which would you prefer?'). These words convey *A*'s genuine desire to understand *B*'s position and his wish for partnership with *B*.

Summary

By checking out his assumption about the meaning of *B*'s frown *A* makes his concern discussable. *B*'s response disconfirms his assumption and enables the conversation to shift its focus and direction, by agreement, towards the implications of *A*'s work for the business plan.

Outcomes

A's open-to-learning approach achieves a number of outcomes that are beneficial.

For A. *A* is left with a clear indication of *B*'s attitude to his plans.

For A and B's relationship. The straight exchange of information in this conversation sets the scene for an ongoing productive working relationship with *B*.

For the organisation. The careful joint consideration that is being given to *A*'s plans can to lead to decisions that will benefit the organisation.

9. Responding to pressure to go beyond what we feel comfortable with (open approach)

B, a member of staff, asks *A*, a new manager, for advice. *A* knows he is not in a position to give advice that might solve *B*'s difficulty because he knows little concerning the situation about which he is being consulted. However, he feels under pressure to offer advice because he thinks that, as a manager, he should be in a position to do this.

How might *A* deal with his difficulty?

A's thoughts	*A* and *B*'s words
	B. I've got a problem in the office. Some of the staff are complaining that they are overworked and that others don't pull their weight. I've tried to explain that it only looks that way because the nature of the work varies from person to person. But there's still a lot of tension. Please tell me what to do!
(1) Oh dear! This could be a tricky problem... I wish I knew a bit more about the office... I really don't know about the different jobs or personalities or even how well *B* manages things. But I am *B*'s line manager now and I should be able to support her by giving her advice...I'm feeling under pressure here...	
I'm feeling under pressure... **alert**... ...**cue**... Remember the principles of open conversation.	
(2) Am I making any assumptions that are making things difficult for me? I can feel that I'm worried about my image as a manager... perhaps I should stop being hung up on my own need to be seen to be the expert on everything *(assumptions)*.	

B needs to know that I don't know the office situation well enough to give quick advice *(information)*. Then we can focus on sorting her problem out.

A. (1) I'd like to be able to offer some advice but I've got a problem. As you know, I'm new to this department and I don't feel I've had a chance to get my head round the office situation yet. I could give you some ideas, based on my past experience, but I'd feel these would be superficial. To be really useful to you I need to find out a bit more about the office situation first.
Can you understand my position?

B. Yes. I realise that you're new to the department but I was hoping you could give me some general ideas.

(3) Mm....*B*'s certainly turning up the pressure ... but I can't give general advice in this situation... I'm still feeling under pressure.

I'm still feeling under pressure...
alert...
...**cue**... Remember the principles of open conversation.

(4) Perhaps I *could* be of some immediate help to *B* without simply telling her what to do *(assumptions)*. *She* knows the situation... perhaps we could go through some of the options and decide together on some next steps *(partnership)*...

A. (2) It sounds as though you are a bit desperate for some advice before I've had a chance to get to know the situation better... I wonder if we could together come up with some steps to take which I could feel confident about? But you would need to realise that because I don't know the situation very well, any ideas I come up with may not

	solve the problem. Would you feel happy with that? *B.* Yes, that would be fine.

A's thoughts and words evaluated in terms of the components of the open-to-learning model

Thoughts (1)

'Oh dear! This could be a tricky problem... I wish I knew a bit more about the office... I really don't know about the different jobs or personalities or even how well *B* manages things. But I am *B*'s line manager now and I should be able to support her by giving her advice... I'm feeling under pressure here...'

'I'm feeling under pressure... **alert**...
...**cue**... Remember the principles of open conversation.'

Alert...cue. *A* identifies feelings of discomfort at being under pressure *(alert)*. He uses these to prompt him to think things through in terms of the three principles before replying *(cue)*, thus avoiding being trapped into giving advice that goes beyond what he is comfortable with.

Thoughts (2)

'Am I making any assumptions that are making things difficult for me? I can feel that I'm worried about my image as a manager... perhaps I should stop being hung up on my own need to be seen to be the expert on everything *(assumptions)*.

'*B* needs to know that I don't know the office situation well enough to give quick advice *(information)*. Then we can focus on sorting her problem out.'

Principle One (Question any relevant assumptions). *A* deals with his unquestioned assumption that, because he is *B*'s line manager he should be able to advise on her problem, by trying to put his assumption on one side ('... perhaps I should stop being hung up on my own need to be seen to be the expert on everything'). In doing so *A* frees himself from feeling the need

191

to give instant advice and is able to think in terms of the other two principles.

Principle Three (Promote the exchange of all relevant information). Principle Three enables *A* to realise that in order to have a well-informed and useful conversation with *B*, he needs to make his difficulty explicit ('He needs to know that I don't know the office situation well enough to give quick advice').

Words (1)

'I'd like to be able to offer some advice but I've got a problem. As you know, I'm new to this department and I don't feel I've had chance to get my head round the office situation yet. I could give you some ideas, based on my past experience, but I'd feel these would be superficial. To be really useful to you I need to find out a bit more about the office situation first.

'Can you understand my position?'

Open advocacy (Advocacy is transparent). *A* acknowledges *B*'s difficulty but also makes clear to *B* that he has a problem (' I'd like to be able to offer immediate advice... but I've got a problem ...'). He makes his advocacy informative in two ways. First, he gives *B* the background to his difficulty ('As you know I'm new to this department...') and second he makes clear his feelings about acceding to *B*'s pressure to give advice ('I'd feel these (ideas) would be superficial'). As a result *B* is likely to feel that her problem has been heard and that *A* is sympathetic to her need to do something about it. Furthermore *B* now has enough information to make it possible for her to understand *A*'s difficulty in offering quick advice.

Open advocacy (Advocacy with inquiry). *A* follows his explanation of his difficulty with a checking question ('Can you understand my position?'). If, in spite of what she has heard, *B* has not fully taken *A*'s situation on board, she is now given the opportunity to let *A* know that. Indeed *B*'s response ('Yes... but...') makes it clear to *A* that, in spite of his full explanation, *B* has not fully appreciated his difficulty.

Thoughts (3)

'Mm....*B*'s certainly turning up the pressure... but I can't give general advice in this situation...

'I'm still feeling under pressure... **alert**...**cue**... Remember the principles of open conversation.'

Alert...cue. **A** identifies that **B**'s reply is putting further pressure on him *(alert)*. He again uses these feelings to prompt him to think things through in terms of the three principles *(cue)*.

Thoughts (4)

'Perhaps I *could* be of some immediate help to **B** without simply telling her what to do *(assumption)*. *She* knows the situation... perhaps we could go through some of the options and decide together on some next steps *(partnership)*...'

Principle One (Question any relevant assumptions). **A** now deals with a new assumption – that because he does not know the situation he is unable to offer any useful advice – by considering an alternative ('Perhaps I could be of some immediate help to **B** without simply telling her what to do').

Principle Two (Promote partnership). Principle Two prompts **A** to think about sorting out the problem in partnership with **B** ('she knows the situation... perhaps we could go through some of the options and decide together on some next steps').

Words (2)

'It sounds as though you are a bit desperate for some advice before I've had chance to get to know the situation better... I wonder if we could together come up with some steps to take which I could feel confident about? But you would need to realise that because I don't know the situation very well, any ideas I come up with may not solve the problem. Would you feel happy with that?'

Open advocacy (Advocacy is transparent). Again **A** acknowledges that he has heard what **B** is saying ('It sounds as though you are a bit desperate for some advice'). However, his words include an explicit reminder to **B** that **A** also has a problem ('... before I've had chance to get to know the situation better'). Thus **B** is likely to feel that she has been sympathetically heard by **A**, as well as being reminded that **A**'s problem also needs to be taken into account.

Open advocacy (Advocacy is transparent). **A**'s next words are couched as a statement of **A**'s thinking ('... I wonder if we could together come up with some steps to take but which I could feel confident about'), on which he then expands (' ... but you would need to realise that because I don't know the situation very well, any ideas I come up with may not solve the problem'). Thus *A* offers *B* a way forward, not necessarily ideal from *B*'s point of view, but based on the reality of the situation.

Open advocacy (Advocacy with inquiry). *A* follows up his extended advocacy with a question ('Would you feel happy with that?') that relates to the whole range of advocacy statements he has made. This question is meant to ascertain whether *B* has taken on board *A*'s difficulty so that they can start work on the problem together.

Summary

Because *A* questions his assumption that as a manager he should be able to offer immediate advice he is able to make his concern about his lack of knowledge discussable. As a result the conversation can move on to consider the best way to tackle *B*'s problem in the light of that fact.

Outcomes

By making first his own uncertainties and then the joint problem discussable, *A* increases the chance of bringing about the following beneficial outcomes.

For A. *A* can feel satisfied that he has done all that it is possible for him to do in the circumstances and that his integrity remains intact.

For A and B's relationship. *A*'s approach suggests that he can be trusted to give soundly based advice, and that he can withstand pressure, while still being able to have a useful dialogue. At the same time, *A*'s invitation to *B* to work in partnership, in a way that takes account of her (*B*'s) better local knowledge, sets the basis for a collaborative working relationship.

For the organisation. Although no decision is made at this point in the conversation, the chances are increased that the problem will be dealt with in a way that is appropriate in the circumstances.

10. Handling a conflict of views between ourselves and another person (open approach)

At a meeting to review allocation of resources, **B**, the Sales Director, puts forward a view that is in complete opposition to the way **A**, the Head of Research and Development, sees things.

How might **A** deal with his difficulty?

A's thoughts	A and B's words
	B. I feel that over the next three years the emphasis should shift decisively towards Sales. We should work towards having a significantly greater number of sales people to increase our share of the market.
(1) This makes me so angry. R&D refines and develops the product – without us there wouldn't be anything to sell. If there are extra resources they should come to us, not be siphoned off to Sales.	
I'm angry… **alert**… …**cue**… Remember the principles of open conversation.	
(2) I'm thinking in terms of 'I'm right. She's wrong'. It's possible that both our views are valid *(assumptions)* and that what we need is a way forward that will take account of both our points of view *(partnership)*. But first I need to let her know my own position *(information)*.	
	A. (1) My own view is that R&D deserves more resources… but it seems to me that we may both have a point. We have to promote and sell our products as you rightly say. At the same time we have to

	have a product that has been soundly developed. I wonder if there is some way we can take both viewpoints into account?
	B. How do you mean?
3) Hmm. I need to make my thinking clearer *(information)*. What I mean is that we have to start by accepting that each of us holds a position that is perfectly valid from our own point of view *(partnership)*.	
	A. (2) Well it seems to me that we both hold different views and we hold them fairly strongly. I think it would be good if we could start by accepting that for each of us, given our particular perspective, those views are reasonable. Is it possible for you to see my views as reasonable?
	B. Well when you put it like that... I don't agree with your views but I can see why you might hold them.
(4) We seem to have a starting point. So how can we find a way forward that will take account of both our points of view? *(partnership)*	
	A. (3) OK.... so is there any way we can approach the problem in a way that takes account of our different perspectives?

A's thoughts and words evaluated in terms of the components of the open-to-learning model

Thoughts (1)

'This makes me so angry. R&D refines and develops the product – without us there wouldn't be anything to sell. If there are extra resources they should come to us, not be siphoned off to Sales.

'I'm angry... **alert**...
...**cue**... Remember the principles of open conversation.'

Alert...cue. **A** identifies his anger at **B**'s words *(alert)* and uses this to prompt him to think things through in terms of the three principles before replying *(cue).* He thus avoids being trapped into simply defending his own position or attacking **B**'s.

Thoughts (2)

'I'm thinking in terms of "I'm right. She's wrong". It's possible that both our views are valid *(assumptions)* and that what we need is a way forward that will take account of both our points of view *(partnership).* But first I need to let her know my own position *(information).*'

Principle One (Question any relevant assumptions). As he listens to **B**'s words, **A** makes an assumption that his own perspective (that the extra resources they should come to his department) is correct and that **B**'s position is wrong. However, prompted by Principle One, **A** manages to put this assumption on one side and to look for an alternative way of seeing things ('I'm thinking in terms of "I'm right, he's wrong". It's possible that both our views are valid'). This new thinking opens up possibilities other than defending his own position or attacking **B**'s.

Principle Two (Promote partnership). Principle Two prompts **A** to look for a shared goal that might foster partnership ('what we need is a way forward that will take account of both our points of view'), and to check **B**'s agreement to this possibility.

Principle Three (Promote the exchange of all relevant information). Principle Three prompts **A** to be explicit about his own views ('But first I need to let her know my own position').

Words (1)

'My own view is that R&D deserves more resources... but it seems to me that we may both have a point. We have to promote and sell our products as you rightly say. At the same time we have to have a product that has been soundly developed. I wonder if there is some way we can take both viewpoints into account?'

Open advocacy (Advocacy is transparent). **A** puts forward his own view – so that **B** knows there is a disagreement. **A** then makes a statement ('we may both have a point') which he further clarifies ('...we have to promote and sell our products as you rightly say... at the same time we have to have a product that has been soundly developed'). **A**'s clarification of the problem is intended to convey that he is treating B's views as being as important as his own.

Open advocacy (Advocacy with inquiry). A combines advocacy and inquiry in his suggestion to B ('I wonder if there is some way we can take both our viewpoints into account?') i.e. 'There may be some way we can take our viewpoints into account *(advocacy)*... can you think of a way?' *(inquiry).* This input is intended to open up for B a productive way of looking at the problem.

Thoughts (3)

'Hmm. I need to make my thinking clearer *(information)*. What I mean is that we have to start by accepting that each of us holds a position that is perfectly valid from our own point of view *(partnership)*.'

Principle Three (Promote the exchange of all relevant information). When B replies, 'What do you mean?', Principle Three prompts A to realise that he needs to be more explicit about his thinking ('I need to make my thinking clearer') – that they hold different points of view...

Principle Two (Promote partnership). ... and that both of these have some validity.

Words (2)

'Well it seems to me that we both hold different views and we hold them fairly strongly. I think it would be good if we could start by accepting that for each of us, given our particular perspective, those views are reasonable. Is it possible for you to see my views as reasonable?'

Open advocacy (Advocacy with inquiry). At this point A makes explicit what has so far been implicit – that there is a conflict of views ('... it seems to me that we both hold different views and we hold them fairly strongly'). A then goes on to expand on his previous suggestion of a way forward ('...I think it would be good if we could both start by accepting that for each of us, given our particular perspective, those views are reasonable'). He follows this with a question to try to elicit feedback from B in response to what he is saying ('Is it possible for you to see my views as reasonable?'). The fact that A has first explained the background to his question increases the likelihood that it will come over as a genuine request for B's views rather than as manipulative (as in: 'I'll get him to admit to that... and therefore he'll have to admit the other... and then I've got him!'). For this reason, *B* is very likely to feel able to give a genuine response.

Thoughts (4)

'We seem to have a starting point. So how can we find a way forward that will take account of both our points of view *(partnership)*?'

Principle Two (Promote partnership in the conversation). A returns to the question of how to promote a conversational partnership with *B*.

Words (1)

'OK.... so is there any way we can approach the problem in a way that takes account of our different perspectives?'

Open inquiry (Inquiry is genuine). A uses the language of 'we' and 'our' to invite *B* into joint problem-solving ('...so is there any way we can approach the problem so that we take account of our different perspectives?'). This is likely to convey that *A* is genuinely looking for a co-operative solution rather than trying to win the argument.

Summary

As in the closed conversational approach, the conflicting concerns of both parties are out in the open from the outset. However, *A*'s explicit acknowledgement of a conflict of views, and his reiteration of the need to see that both their points of view have validity, help to make the difficulties discussable. This opens the way for resolving the allocation of resources in a way that is acceptable to both *A* and *B* and in a way that is likely to lead to a win-win situation.

Outcomes

For A. A is likely to feel that he has done all he can to avoid an unproductive argument with B.

For A and B's relationship. The scene is set for the possibility of a co-operative working relationship between *A* and *B*.

For the organisation. If the allocation of resources is made on the basis of co-operation between two managers this is likely to produce maximum benefit to the organisation.

10

Using the Open-to-Learning Approach

Learning points

We can draw on the open-to-learning model to deal with whatever difficulties may come up in a conversation.

The strategy of alert & cue can help us sustain an open-to-learning approach *throughout* a conversation.

So far, in Part Three, we have described the main components of the open-to-learning model and illustrated these through ten annotated conversations. In this chapter we look at how we might put the open-to-learning model into practice in the context of an extended conversation during which we may encounter more than one type of difficulty.

The last chapter (and also Chapter 5) covered ten conversations, each dealing with one specific type of difficulty. However, in practice we are often confronted with a number of such difficulties during the course of a single conversation. It is in this kind of situation that the strength of the open-to-learning model becomes most apparent, because it does not necessitate us racking our brains to remember a host of 'useful' but unrelated 'tips' about how to handle these difficulties. Instead, we can draw on the comprehensive but concise model of open conversation, its three principles and two forms of words, and on the useful strategy of 'alert and cue' for making the transition from closed to open.

This chapter describes and annotates an extended example of a difficult conversation at work[11]. The conversation is between a headteacher (**A**) and

---

[11] The words of this extended conversation have been taken from the training video 'Tackling Tough Issues' (Robinson and Absolum, 1988). We have supplied the head teacher's thoughts.

her Head of Science (**B**). In our analysis we focus on the headteacher's thoughts and words. The difficulties she faces include seven of those illustrated in the ten types of difficult conversation set out in Chapter 1. The numbers in brackets, below and in the annotated rounds of conversation, refer to these ten types of difficulty.

In the order they appear in the conversation, these difficulties are as follows:

- Responding to pressure to go beyond what we feel comfortable with (Conversation No. 9).
- Handling a conflict of views (Conversation No. 10).
- Communicating unwelcome information (Conversation No. 2).
- Engaging with someone who will not discuss things with us (Conversation No. 5).
- Dealing with a conflict of loyalties (Conversation No. 6).
- Responding to non-verbal behaviour that bothers us (Conversation No. 8).
- Coping with being criticised (Conversation No. 7).

It is important to note that **A** does not need to distinguish each type of difficulty as it presents itself. All she needs to do is to remember the three principles of open conversation, and the forms of words that derive from these. She can then use the awareness-raising strategy, alert & cue (described in Chapter 8), as often as necessary to enable her to put the open-to-learning model into practice at each turn of the conversation. In this way difficulties become discussable and are dealt with effectively as they arise.

   In order to match our annotations to the text, we present the conversation one 'round' at a time. Each round consists of **B**'s words, **A**'s thoughts and **A**'s words, with footnotes showing each different type of difficulty as it arises. Our comments on each round indicate how **A**'s use of the open conversation approach enables her to deal with a work issue in a way that maintains a positive working relationship with **B** and can bring benefits to the organisation (the school) as a whole.

Using the open-to-learning approach in an extended difficult conversation: an annotated example

Setting: After considerable discussion, the staff of a secondary school have devised a committee procedure for approving class trips and out of school activities.

In this extended conversation, *B*, the head of science, urgently wants to see *A*, the head teacher, because he believes the committee, in the light of the agreed procedure, will not be able to consider his application for a class trip in time for him to make the arrangements that will be necessary.

A's thoughts	*A* and *B*'s words
Round One I remember him telling me about this last week. I'm glad we've got a committee to deal with this sort of thing. So I wonder why he's coming to me? He can be such a bully. I'm worried that he wants me to go over the committee's head in some way...* I'm feeling worried... **alert**... ...**cue**... Remember the principles of open conversation. ...but I could be wrong. Better not prejudge things. I'll hear what he has to say. I'll let him know that I remember our earlier conversation and then take it from there.	*B*. ... I wanted to talk to you about the third year field trip to the coast. *A*. Ah, yes. That's the one you were talking to me about the other day.

* Responding to pressure to go beyond what we feel comfortable with (Conversation 9)

A notes her negative feelings ('I'm feeling worried') (*alert*), and lets this *cue* her into using the three principles. Using *Principle One*, *A* is able to put on one side her untested assumption that *B* wants her to go over the committee's head. This enables her to avoid being limited by closed thinking, and to communicate to **B** that the topic he has introduced is one

Round Two	
	B. Right. OK. Have you got the go-ahead yet?
What does he mean, have I got the go ahead? He must know it's the committee's job and that they don't meet till next week ... so there can't have been a decision... but he's acting as though he didn't know this. How annoying...	
I can feel myself getting annoyed... **alert**... ...**cue**... Remember the principles of open conversation.	
...but perhaps he didn't know about the committee's role. He may not like it but I'd better give him the facts that there's been no decision made yet, and why this is.	
	A. No, no I haven't, because that's handled by a committee now and they're not meeting until the end of next week.

she remembers *(Principle Three).*

Having dealt with her untested assumption in Round One, *A* again finds herself needing to repeat the *alert & cue* process in order to prevent her annoyance from pushing her back into a closed position. This time it is her assumption that *B* is not being straight about what he knows that she puts on one side *(Principle One)*. This enables her to ignore any suspicion that *B* is being disingenuous and allows her to communicate information about the role of the committee in the spirit of information exchange *(Principle Three)*.

A's open thinking and open form of words work towards partnership in the discussion *(Principle Two)* by ensuring that she and *B* share the same facts about the committee. If *B* did not know the facts before this, he does so now.

Round Three	**B.** Till the end of *next* week!
He sounds aggrieved......I'm aggrieved too! As if it were my fault that the committee's doesn't meet until next week!	
I'm feeling annoyed again... **alert**... ...**cue**... Remember the principles of open conversation.	
....best to ignore that – who knows what he's thinking – and just confirm the facts.	
	A. Yes. That's right.

For a third time **A** finds herself identifying negative feelings and preventing herself being driven by them *(alert & cue)*. She goes through the cycle of putting untested assumptions about **B**'s thinking to one side ('best to ignore that...') *(Principle One)*, and continues with her communication of relevant information in response to **B**'s comment *(Principle Three)*.

Round Four	**B.** Well that causes me a bit of a problem because I'm going to need a decision by the end of *this* week. In fact the trip goes in ten days time and I've got to confirm the booking. I've also got to book the buses and confirm with the parents and so on, so I really need a decision by Friday at the latest
He does seem to be in real difficulties. I need to be clear that I've fully understood his problem. I'll check.	
	A. Ah...so you're saying that the committee is actually meeting to make its decision too late for you to get the trip organised?

Because of the way that **A** has maintained openness in her thinking, she has put herself into a position where she is able to 'hear' what **B** is trying to communicate to her and respond to his problem on its merits. She thus avoids being sidetracked by any closed thoughts and, for instance, defending the new committee procedure. Checking her understanding of **B**'s words *(advocacy with inquiry)* clarifies the issue. It also invites partnership by communicating to **B** that he has been heard, and that she is prepared to take account of his thinking in the ongoing discussion *(Principle Two)*.

Round Five	
	B. It looks that way...yes.
So I was understanding him correctly. But it presents a problem for me too... for both of us in fact. I'm caught between the needs of the children and supporting the committee procedures.*	
I'm feeling caught... **alert**... ...**cue**... Remember the principles of open conversation.	
Perhaps there is a possibility of sorting this out in a way that takes care of both the children's needs and the committee procedures.	
	A. Oh. Well let's take a look at this.
	(Pause for thought)

*Dealing with a conflict of loyalties (Conversation 6)

By recognizing her negative feelings ('being caught between the needs of the children and supporting the committee procedures'), and avoiding being driven by them *(alert & cue)*, **A** has managed to accommodate **B**'s problem as well as to her own. As a result, **A** is now able to think in terms of partnership – how to meet both **A** and **B**'s needs rather than allowing one of them to 'win' at the expense of the other *(Principle Two)*. Her words are an invitation to **B** to work with her in finding a solution to what, at this point, appears to her to be a shared view of the problem *(inquiry is genuine)*. So far they seem to be on course for a discussion in partnership about an agreed problem.

Round Six	
	B. What I need from you is the go-ahead now. We can square it with the committee afterwards.

It doesn't sound as though he's in the business of solving the problem in way that suits us both! It sound like he's not interested in the committee and he's not going to like the fact that I'm not prepared to bypass it. This is tiresome.*

I'm feeling impatient... **alert**...
...**cue**... Remember the principles of open conversation.

Maybe he really doesn't realise the problem it will create for me. I need to make that clear before we can tackle the trip issue.

A. Well that causes me a bit of a problem, because we've spent...and I actually was very much involved in this...some time setting up a committee procedure so that staff could check with one another about field trips and taking students off campus before they went away...and I'm really quite reluctant to undermine those procedures.

*Handling a conflict of views (Conversation 10)
Communicating unwelcome information (Conversation 2)

B's reply now suggests that he is not working in partnership on a shared problem as *A* is trying to do, and that he is only interested in solving that aspect of the problem that concerns him. Not only does he not agree to joint problem-solving, he demands his own solution.

Once again, *A*'s *alertness* to her negative feeling ('I'm feeling impatient') *cues* her into the three principles. This has two positive effects: first, it prevents her from being driven by her assumption that *B* is ignoring her difficulty *(Principle One)*, and from responding in a closed way to what seems to be a conflict of views and the pressure *B* is putting on her; second, it allows her to consider an alternative interpretation of *B*'s reasons for pressing his case – that *B* may not fully understand her position *(Principle One)*.

As a next step, therefore, she does all she can to establish that *B* really does understand her dilemma, since, however much he may dislike it, without a shared understanding of the problem they stand no chance of making their discussion about the trip a partnership *(Principle Two)*. *A* makes sure that she gives **B** all the information that is relevant *(Principle Three)*, including her own part in setting up the committee ('and I actually was very much involved in this') and her commitment to it ('and I'm really quite reluctant to undermine those procedures') *(advocacy is transparent)*.

Round Seven	
	B. But I mean, who's going to object to this trip? I mean the kids are keen to go, the Science Department's in favour, I've checked with the parents, I've got all those consent forms signed…
Not very successful! He's still only seeing it from his point of view… which is a fair one… but I'm puzzled as to how this whole issue arose in the first place when we now have a perfectly good committee procedure in place. Was he late in applying or something? I'll ask, and explain why I want to know.	
	A. I acknowledge that it probably is a pretty good thing that you're proposing, and I also acknowledge your problem…in that we now seem to be short of time in terms of your planning. But I'm wondering if this problem has arisen because you applied late. Can I ask you, when did you put in your application?

B's comment ('But I mean…') indicates that **A**'s attempts to communicate her difficulty have not succeeded. **B** is still not taking **A**'s position on board and showing willingness to discuss it. He is simply continuing to press his case. At this point, rather than repeating her own position, **A** decides that she needs to explore **B**'s situation further in her continuing attempt to bring any relevant issues or difficulties into the open so that they can be discussed *(Principles Two and Three)*.

By explaining why she wants to know when **B** put in his application ('I'm wondering if this problem has arisen because you applied late'), **A** makes clear to B that her inquiry ('Can I ask you, when did you put in your application?') is a genuine request for information and not, for example, a way of trying to catch him out *(inquiry with advocacy)*.

207

Rounds Eight, Nine and Ten	*B*. Er... it was the beginning of last week.
Ah so that's what has created the problem. I'll let him know I'm still following him.	
	A. OK. So in fact your application missed the earlier committee.
	B. Yes... but there was a good reason for that. There was a cancellation at the Education Centre and this was too good an opportunity to miss.
A missing bit of information! I'll let him know I'm following him.	
	A. Oh I see. So it came up at the last minute.
	B. Yes. And if I don't take it now I'm going to lose it.
Another bit of the jigsaw. Where do we go from here? The trip sounds good. But on the other hand if I pre-empt the committee, that's going to undermine all our attempts to make this school one in which people have a say in things that affect them. I'll put both viewpoints to him and see if we can solve the problem in a way that suits us both.	
	A. Right. OK. Well from my perspective I think there are two issues and I'd like to keep...

As a result of her inquiry, *A* achieves three rounds of cooperative and useful discussion. Her exploration of the background to the dilemma appears to have been effective in that she has been able to elicit from *B* further information that increases her own understanding of the situation ('...there was a good reason for that. There was a cancellation at the Education Centre and this was too good an opportunity to miss... if I don't take it now I'm going to lose it'). She has also been able to let *B* know that she has heard what he is saying – and has checked that she has understood him correctly – by putting those concerns into her own words ('So in fact your application missed the earlier committee', 'so it came up at the last minute') *(Principle Two and Principle Three)*.

With **B**'s new information on the table, she has created what seems to be a well-informed, shared basis for partnership in the discussion *(Principle Two)*. Because she has managed to remain open, **A** is able to see her divided loyalties between the pupils' educational opportunities and the requirements of the committee as a problem to be solved, rather than feeling that she has to come down on one side or the other.

Round Eleven	
	B. No. The only issue is the educational value for the children. Come on ...
	... it's central to the course, it's going to improve their chances in the exams.
He's so intent on getting what he wants that he really isn't interested in my concerns about the committee. He's still trying to bully me with his arguments. That's just not on and I'm starting to feel annoyed again.*	
I'm feeling annoyed again... **alert**... ...**cue**... Remember the principles of open conversation.	
Before I let him go any further I should check whether I'm right in thinking that he's quite prepared to see me undermine the committee procedures.	
	A. **B**, I'm going to interrupt you because I see you as asking me to undermine the procedures...

*Engaging with someone who will not discuss things with us. (Conversation 5)

B's response suggests that **A**'s efforts to establish common ground have again reached an impasse. Although **A** has made it clear that she understands **B**'s problem, **B** is still unwilling to acknowledge hers. Preparedness to discuss and flexibility is still one-sided.

Triggered by her annoyance *(alert)* **A** looks again to the three principles for guidance *(cue)*. She identifies her assumption that **B** expects her to undermine the committee procedures, and decides to check it out directly with **B** *(Principle One)* in order to make sure that she is accurate in her understanding of **B**'s thinking ('I see you as asking me to undermine the procedures...'). In doing so she puts her difficulty on the table, making it clear that this is how she interprets *B*'s attitude. This makes it difficult for him to continue to avoid the issue of the committee's involvement.

Round Twelve Maybe I was wrong, and he isn't asking me to undermine the committee. But the speeding up idea has some merit. We don't have a procedure for more urgent decisions at present and perhaps we should. I'll let him know that finding a means of speeding things up could be a way to solve his problem. But I still have to make sure that he takes the responsibilities of the committee seriously. It may help if I spell out the consequences of not doing so.	*B*. No, not undermine. I just want you to speed things up. I need a decision. *A*. OK. I think there may be ways I can speed things up and I'd like to tell you what they might be… but I want to find a way of doing that without undermining that committee procedure because I as a head teacher am going to lose credibility fast if I start undermining the committee procedures in this school.

A's checking out has helped *B* to communicate what he *does* want – to speed things up rather than undermining the committee *(Principle Three)*. *A* now sees *B*'s words as offering a basis for discussion. She tries to strengthen this understanding with *B* by letting him know that she intends to follow up the idea ('I think there may be ways I can speed things up and I'd like to tell you what they might be').

At the same time however, *A* still feels some doubts as to whether, in spite of his words, *B* really does take the committee procedures seriously and whether they actually do have a true basis for discussion and negotiation. Rather than ignore this doubt, she attempts to make sure that *B* really has all the information he needs *(Principle Three)* in order to take her problem (the need to go through the committee) seriously.

A therefore repeats her message and reinforces it by giving *B* further information about the likely consequences, for her and for the school, if the committee is ignored *(advocacy is transparent)*.

Round Thirteen	(*B* curls his lip)
That looked like a sneer. Doesn't my credibility count? He's putting me down and that makes me angry.*	
I feel angry... **alert**... ...**cue**... Remember the principles of open conversation.	
Whatever his expression it doesn't necessarily mean that he hasn't taken my problem on board. I'll reiterate that we need to look for a solution that we are both happy with and try not to react to the way he looks.	
	A.... so I'd like to see if we can find a way that fast tracks things for you without undermining those procedures.

*Responding to non-verbal behaviour that bothers us. (Conversation 8)

B's facial expression suggests to *A* that *B* is sneering at her and that her words are indeed being ignored. However, *A* is able to use the anger that her sense of being put down produces *(alert)* to *cue* her into the three principles for a seventh time. As a result, she puts her initial reaction to *B*'s non-verbal behaviour on one side *(Principle One)*. In doing so she prevents herself from falling back into closed behaviour, which might lead her to offer further repetitions of her own position. This enables her to suggest a common goal that takes account of both their positions *(Principle Two)*. Note that she fails to add any inquiry here. By not following up her advocacy with an inquiry that checks *B*'s reaction to her suggestion *(advocacy without inquiry)*, she is unlikely to get a reply that lets her know what *B* thinks of her idea.

Round Fourteen	*B*. I mean they're going to approve this trip anyway. Why can't we just go ahead?
At least he's acknowledging that the committee is part of the picture but he seems to see their role as just applying a rubber stamp. I can't leave	

him with that impression or the authority of the committee in the school would be undermined. I need to make clear that the committee's approval is not a foregone conclusion and that we still have a problem.	
	A. They *may* approve it, **B**, but it's the job of the committee to make the decision and I don't want to pre-empt that decision.

Because *A* did not check his reaction to what she said, *B* is able easily to ignore her last comment and continue to pursue his own agenda. His response implies that he still only partly appreciates (or is prepared to acknowledge) that the committee's role is not just to rubber stamp decisions made by the head. *A* therefore decides to spell this out ('They *may* approve it, *B*, but...') *(Principle Three)*.

Round Fifteen	**B.** It's crazy! The decision shouldn't be down to them anyway. This is a science trip and it should be organised by the science department and that's all the approval we need. If the parents are in favour of the trip and the kids want to go I don't see what it's to do with anyone else.
Wow. That's what he really thinks of the committee! So there is another problem for me to deal with. He's criticising the committee structure I was involved in setting up. I feel angry about that.*	
I'm feeling angry... **alert**... ...**cue**... Remember the principles of open conversation.	
Actually I could be wrong...he may have valid reasons for disliking the committee's remit to deal with these matters. But this isn't the time to go into details. I'll let him know I think that	

his views on the committee's remit may be legitimate but that I'll need to deal with that at another time.	
	A. OK. I now see a third problem which is that you have some questions about the authority of the committee itself… and that also may be a legitimate concern. But I'd really like to try and keep the issue of the trip and the committee's role separate, because I'm going to get in a real muddle if we don't.

* Coping with being criticised (Conversation 7)

Although *A*'s suggestion of an agreed way forward has so far been ignored, her persistence in trying to achieve a shared understanding of the problem (rather than allowing herself to be browbeaten into submitting to *B*'s pressure) eventually induces *B* to disclose information about his position that he has so far not raised. Although this new information presents *A* with a previously unforeseen issue, it makes a useful contribution to her understanding of *B*'s problem. Because this new problem is now on the table, it can become the subject of ongoing discussion.

A is angered by this new information that criticises the committee system by questioning its authority *(alert)*. However she is able to deal with her reaction by using her anger to *cue* her once again into the three principles. This enables her to put to one side her negative judgement of *B*'s opinion by entertaining the possibility that he may have a point *(Principle One)*. She is thus in a position to let *B* know this, and in this way make a further contribution to the conversation becoming a partnership *(Principle Two)*. At the same time she recognises that she is unable to deal effectively with all the issues now on the table. She therefore communicates this concern to *B* and lets him know how she proposes to deal with it. By giving *B* her reason for wanting to keep the two issues separate ('because I'm going to get in a real muddle if we don't') *A* makes her *advocacy transparent*.

Round Sixteen	
	B. It seems to me that this is just a recipe for slowing things down. It's a recipe for not getting things done! They're going to defer it... it's going to go on and on...
It's the old bureaucracy argument. But we still need to come back to the main issue. I'll suggest a way forward for the immediate problem that also takes account of all the issues that have come up.	
	A. I think we need to find a way whereby the committee can be able to let people like you take advantage of opportunities at the last minute. And maybe we don't have that procedure at the moment. And I'd like to talk with the chair of the committee about how we can find...

B has apparently not heard *A*'s acknowledgement of his problem with the committee because he continues to complain. However, because *A* has worked so hard to elicit all relevant aspects of *B*'s thinking *(Principle Three)*, she now finds herself in a position to suggest a way forward that takes into account all the issues that have been aired by both sides *(Principle Two)*: *B*'s wish to get the go-ahead for the trip in spite of his late application, his misgivings about the committee's procedures and *A*'s own concern not to bypass the committee.

Round Seventeen	
	B. When will you be able to do that?
He's hearing me at last. Perhaps now, between us all, we'll find a solution to the problem of the trip... and it's been helpful to identify that we need a fast-track procedure for the committee. I'll let him know my view that the committee chair should be brought in as soon as possible – and that I'd like him to be part of the discussion if he wants to be.	
	A. I would like to see the chair of the committee with you... if you want to come with me?...in fact I'd like you to...

B's response suggests that *A*'s formulation of a way forward that takes account of all his concerns has at last brought *B* to a reluctant acceptance that he has to take account, not only of his own urgent requirements, but also of *A*'s need to consult the committee. By focusing on their joint concerns *(Principle Two) A* has put herself and *B* in a position to make these concerns discussable. She reinforces once again that she sees the way forward as a partnership *(Principle Two)* by inquiring whether *B* would like to accompany her in talking to the chair of the committee ('...in fact I'd like you to...') *(inquiry with advocacy)*.

Outcomes of an open-to-learning approach to the extended conversation

By the end of this conversation, the only decision that has been made is to take all the issues to the committee. The outcome of further discussions about the trip is open-ended. Nevertheless, *A*'s approach to the conversation has already produced a number of beneficial outcomes:

For A. *A* can justifiably feel that she has managed to fulfil her responsibilities as headteacher effectively by reconciling her desire to support a school-wide initiative with *B*'s demand for a quick decision.

For A's relationship with B. *A* has conducted the conversation in a way that suggests that she and *B* will continue to be able to talk to one another as partners in the conversation in the future. *B* has learnt that *A* cannot be bullied and that, at the same time, his own views have been listened to and taken into account – and that this is likely to be the case in future encounters.

For the school. With *B*'s agenda (to get his urgent concerns met without the committee's involvement) dealt with, and both *A* and **B**'s difficulties acknowledged, the likelihood of achieving an effective discussion with the committee in the future is greatly enhanced. There is now a real possibility that a solution to *B*'s problem will be found that does not ignore the committee and its procedures. At the same time, *A*'s open-to-learning approach has brought about new learning – that there may be a problem with the committee's procedure that needs reviewing. Additionally *A*'s authority as head teacher, and her reputation for demonstrating respect for her staff, and working hard at artnership with them, has been reinforced.

PART FOUR

The Organisational Context and Closed and Open-to-Learning Approaches to Difficult Conversations

11

Difficult Conversations that Stem from the Workplace and Its Culture

Learning points

There is a class of assumptions that represents closed interpretations of the values ('social virtues') that organisations espouse.

When such assumptions are unquestioned and widely held by individuals within an organisation, they can impact negatively on our handling of difficult conversations.

These kinds of assumption can create particular difficulties concerning:

- what can or cannot be spoken about.
- conversations between people of different status.

Managers are in a strong position to help those they manage to become more open-to-learning.

~~~~~~~~~~~~~~~~

Through two exercises we invite you to evaluate any mismatches between the espoused values of your organisation and how people behave in practice, and between your own espoused values and your own practice.

</div>

In this chapter, we turn our attention to the organisational context in which difficult conversations at work take place. In particular we look at how unquestioned assumptions that are widely held within an organisation can have a negative effect on the way we handle our difficult conversations.

An important class of these assumptions consists of the way in which individuals interpret the espoused values of the organisation within which they work. Argyris calls such values 'social virtues' (1990 p.19). We argue that social virtues are typically interpreted in closed-to-learning ways and that whether or not we question these interpretations will significantly affect how we manage difficult conversations in the workplace.

Closed and open interpretations of 'social virtues' and their effect on difficult conversations

Over recent decades, many organisations have espoused mission statements that subscribe to social virtues like 'Respect', 'Support', 'Strength', 'Honesty' and 'Integrity'. Such mission statements describe how organisations expect their employees to act in their relationships with one another, with other organisations and with the general public, in the belief that this will bring about beneficial outcomes such as learning and trust.

For example, mission statements often include such aspirations as:

- 'We treat every person as important and of value.' *(Respect)*
- 'We are allowed to learn from our mistakes.' *(Support)*
- 'We talk to one another in an open way.' *(Honesty)*

We find, however, that there is typically a mismatch between the aspirational values of an organisation, embodied in their mission statement, and the closed-to-learning culture that exists in practice. The reason we say this is because one of the exercises we have given practitioners attending our courses and workshops is to rate the extent to which the value statements made by their organisation (in their mission statements) are reflected in the way in which people actually relate to one another. Our finding has consistently been that people perceive a clear mismatch between the two. Practitioners were frequently able to cite occasions when the social virtues their organisations espoused, such as that of *Respect* ('We treat every person as important and of value') or *Honesty* ('We talk to one another in an open way'), were not in evidence.

Figure 11.1 is adapted from the work of Argyris (1990, pp. 106-107) and shows how five social virtues can be interpreted in a closed or open way. The interpretations shown in the centre column are generated by closed-to-learning thinking. The interpretations in the right-hand column follow from thinking that is open-to-learning.

Social Virtues	Closed -to-learning	Open-to-learning
Respect	Ensure that authority is respected, including your own, by not challenging those directly above you and not concerning yourself with the views of people below you.	Credit others (both above and below you) with the capacity to question their own actions and ideas responsibly. Be prepared to do the same yourself.
Support	Be supportive when someone gets into difficulties by offering compliments and comfort to make them feel good about themselves, or by agreeing that others are to blame. Avoid questioning their actions in case they become upset.	When someone gets into difficulties, help them to confront their own feelings, assumptions and behaviour.
Strength	Be firm and assertive. Showing doubt is a sign of weakness, so give the impression that you know what you are doing even if you are uncertain.	Have the courage to declare and explain your own position while actively encouraging others to question it too. Be open to consider criticism, even if you feel vulnerable.
Honesty	*Either* tell no lies but reveal no more than is expedient *or* alternatively make your position clear to everyone by sparing none of the details.	Encourage yourself and others to disclose all relevant information, including what people may be afraid to speak openly about. Minimise distortion and avoid exaggeration.
Integrity	Stick rigidly to your principles, values and beliefs whatever the situation.	Advocate your principles, values and beliefs in a way that invites inquiry into them, and encourages other people to do the same.

Figure 11.1 Social virtues: closed-to-learning and open-to-learning interpretations

To examine how the closed and open interpretations of the social virtues apply to your own organisation, we suggest that you try the following exercise.

Exercise:

Evaluating any mismatches between the social virtues your organisation espouses and how people behave in practice

Take each of the social virtues in Figure.11.1 in turn and relate it to the organisation in which you work. Place a tick against whichever interpretative statement (or part of a statement) best matches the *espoused* values of your organisation and a cross against the statement or part of a statement that reflects the way people *actually behave*. Look for any mismatches – cases where any one social virtue has a tick in the right hand column (for an espoused value that is open), and a cross in the centre column (for behaviour that is closed).

While we might expect or hope to find organisational values interpreted in the open-to-learning ways shown on the right of Figure 11.1, the work of Argyris (1990), and the feedback we have had from practitioners, is that, in practice, the closed interpretation of the social virtues are commonplace in organisational life. Why might this be so?

We have stated in previous chapters that closed-to-learning thinking is the 'default condition' for individuals. It is not surprising, therefore, that it is the closed-to-learning interpretation of social virtues described above, interpretations that discourage partnership and the exchange of relevant information, that most frequently determine our actions. We may aspire to act in accordance with the (open) social virtues, but fail to do so because we do not have access to an alternative, open model and the associated skills to make this possible. Because we do not realise that we are driven by a closed-to-learning model, acting *in the name of* the social virtues can lead us to believe that ways of acting towards one another that are actually closed-to-learning are appropriate.

For example, we convince ourselves that 'It wouldn't be *respectful* to challenge my manager' (even though I think he is making a mistake). We believe that 'I was only being *honest*' (even though my opinion was not asked for). We contend that 'I give her all the *support* I can' (when we are afraid to let her know that we believe she is wrong). Such closed-to-learning interpretations of social virtues function as assumptions. Because everyone in the organisation is very likely to be in closed mode, this kind of assumption will be equally likely to be widespread in the culture of the organisation. This, in turn, means that they are rarely questioned by us or by others. Closed-to-learning interpretations of social virtues, therefore, add to our problem of making difficulties discussable.

Examples

Conversation 1 ('Saying something critical'), Chapter 5 page 79.
A manager is worried about saying something critical to an employee because 'there's no way she could cope' (closed interpretation of the social virtue of *Support*) and therefore fails to give the employee the feedback she asks for.

Conversation 4 ('Retrieving a setback in an interpersonal relationship'), Chapter 5 page 90.
A manager feels uncomfortable about putting right bad feelings which have been brought about by her abrupt treatment of a member of staff because 'it doesn't look good for a manager to apologise or admit blame' (closed interpretation of *Strength*). As a result the bad feelings are likely to continue.

Closed interpretations of social virtues within the workplace culture bring about a negative cycle in which they reinforce and perpetuate the closed-to-learning behaviour of individuals – a cycle that becomes self-maintaining and increasingly hard to break.

Example
In a regular business meeting of practitioners, a number of strong-minded individuals would consistently try to 'win' their argument by being assertive and showing little interest in the contribution of others

(closed interpretation of *Strength*). The climate of mutual distrust and suspicion that this closed-to-learning behaviour created gave rise to the widespread assumption that the only way to be heard was to be dominant, assertive and closed to the concerns of others. New staff quickly learned to interact in the same way (assertively and unilaterally), with the result that the closed-to-learning cycle was perpetuated.

Aspects of organisational life where closed interpretations of social virtues create particular pressures

There are a number of areas of organisational life where assumptions based on closed interpretations of social virtues that are widespread in the culture can make it particularly hard for individuals to manage their difficult conversations. We illustrate this point with reference to two of these areas:

- Where there is tacit consensus within an organisation that certain issues cannot be spoken about.
- Where there are widespread assumptions within the organisation (based on closed-to-learning interpretations of the social virtues)about how people of different status should relate to one another.

For both these areas, we will illustrate how a closed interpretation of the social virtues can make difficult conversations hard to handle. We will then discuss ways in which an open interpretation of the social virtues can challenge a prevailing closed culture and foster support within the culture for managing our difficult conversations in an open-to-learning way.

Where there is tacit consensus within an organisation that certain issues cannot be spoken about

Received wisdom stemming from a closed interpretation of social virtues can influence what can and cannot be discussed. Maxims such as 'Don't show doubt' (the social virtue of *Strength*), 'Don't question other people's actions' *(Support), or* 'Say only what is expedient' *(Honesty)* can lead to difficult issues being seen as too delicate or sensitive to raise, so they are avoided.

Example

Everyone in a team that worked closely together was aware that one member of staff was not very good at her job. However, because they wanted to be supportive (closed interpretation of the social virtue of *Support*), no-one raised the issue in a forum that might have enabled it to be dealt with helpfully. Instead, the team simply gossiped about the problem in private, while continuing to live with the negative consequences of carrying a weak team member. They sometimes tried to help the team member out but, in so doing, still failed to face up to the difficulty.

The consensus amongst the team not to raise the problem so that it could be dealt with is tacit rather than discussed, and the problem is covered up. This means that the team consensus is itself protected from challenge. Thus the situation is 'self-sealed' (Argyris 1974 pp.76-77) against any possibility of learning and change.

In this situation, the open-to-learning approach can offer insights and skills that can make the problem discussable. For a problem to be discussable it must be possible for all difficulties to be raised and for all relevant information to be on the table *(Principle Three)*. In this way, the closed interpretation of *Support* can be challenged, the tacit consensus made explicit and the difficulty effectively dealt with.

The following examples are drawn from the open-to-learning versions of the ten types of difficult conversation (Chapter 9).

Examples

Conversation 3 ('Saying something that you believe will go against group consensus'), Chapter 9 Page 166.
Here, the principles and skills of open conversation enable a section manager to voice his dissatisfaction with the conduct of a routine meeting, even though he thinks this will go against the tacit consensus of the rest of the group and that his colleagues will, therefore, react badly. Because his thinking is open-to-learning, he recognises that he is making assumptions about how his colleagues will react. Using the open approach, he opts to present the issue openly, explicitly and as *his* problem (an open interpretation of the social virtues of *Honesty* and *Strength*). This means that the section manager's belief in a tacit group consensus can be checked out publicly and enables him to discover whether or not other people do in fact share his dissatisfaction with the meetings.

Conversation 4 ('Retrieving a setback in an interpersonal relationship'), Chapter 9 page 169.
In this situation, awareness of the principles of open conversation enables a manager to talk to her junior colleague about an earlier incident that had raised bad feelings. She is able to recognise and question her assumption – based on a closed interpretation of the social virtues – that it does not look good for managers to apologise or admit blame, and invite a discussion of what happened (an open interpretation of *Strength*). In doing so she enables any misunderstandings or bad feelings to surface and be dealt with jointly.

Where there are widespread assumptions within the organisation (based on closed-to-learning interpretations of the social virtues) about how people of different status should relate to one another

It is often hard for practitioners to handle difficult conversations effectively when these involve talking to someone in their organisation who they regard as being senior or junior to themselves. Sometimes such imbalances of power can lead to the practitioner feeling that they are being talked down to, or unduly deferred to. For example, it can be difficult to talk in partnership with a manager who silences critical comment by inappropriate exercise of his authority, an administrator who is unduly subservient, a medical practitioner who puts herself in a power-up position by withholding relevant information, or a parent who is nervous about talking to her child's teacher.

Example
On one of our courses, we presented the difficulty dealt with in Conversation 5 of our ten types of difficult conversations ('Responding to someone who refuses to discuss things with you', Chapter 5, page 93) to a team of senior support staff in local government. This is the situation where a hard-pressed administrative assistant is 'yet again' put under pressure by her senior manager to take on extra work that the latter deems to be 'urgent'. On past experience, the administrative assistant believes it will be pointless to say 'no' to this imposition as her boss never seems to take her problem seriously.

We found that, in considering a similar situation at their own place of work, all the senior support staff on our course shared the administrative assistant's unquestioned and organisation-wide assumption that there was no point in saying 'no' to a senior manager who kept on imposing an additional workload. They were strongly of

226

the opinion that challenging their own senior manager's imposition of an additional workload would lead to them being punished or 'got at' in some way. Comments made included: 'They'll put you down as a trouble-maker'; 'You'll be passed over for promotion'; or even, 'You could lose your job'. It was a view they maintained despite the fact that none of them had actually experienced such consequences themselves or known of anyone who had.

Unquestioned assumptions by support staff about how their managers would behave in difficult circumstances reflected a team culture characterised by a closed interpretation of the social virtue of *Respect*. People deferred to those above them in the organisational hierarchy rather than 'crediting their managers with the capacity to question their own actions and ideas' (Figure 11.1). The support staff also held the assumption, based on a closed interpretation of the social virtue *Respect*, that they would be punished in some way if they challenged those above them. This assumption, widely held within their organisation, imposed a blanket constraint on what they felt able to say to a manager in the type of situation illustrated above. It perpetuated their own closed-to-learning stance, thus weakening their ability to deal with similar situations in the future. As a result they put themselves in a position where they had little chance of improving the situation in which they found themselves.

The next example illustrates an open-to-learning approach to the difficulty described above, one that also reflects an open-to-learning interpretation of *Respect*.

Example

Conversation 5 ('Engaging with someone who will not discuss things with you'), Chapter 9 page173)
In this scenario, a senior manager, in his customary way, tries to use his superior status both to give an administrative assistant more urgent work and to ignore her statements that she is unable to cope with the increased workload. By putting herself in open mode, the administrative assistant is able to consider the possibility that, despite past evidence to the contrary, her manager can be persuaded to listen to her. She makes her problem explicit (an open interpretation of *Honesty*) and also makes clear to her manager that there might be adverse consequences for him (an open interpretation of *Respect*) if he does not involve himself in moderating her workload. The administrative assistant's open interpretations enable her to make her issue discussable with her senior in a way that acknowledges his status and maintains good working relationships.

The open model encourages members of an organisation to question any assumption within the culture of the organisation that could inhibit conversations being made a partnership *(Principle Two)*. This includes questioning closed interpretations of the social virtues. The more, therefore, that members of an organisation have the courage and ability to operate from an open-to-learning position, the more likely it becomes that closed-to-learning interpretations of social virtues such as *Respect* come to acquire new open-to-learning meanings within their organisational culture. In this way the culture is able to support (rather than inhibit) its members in managing their difficult conversations in open-to-learning ways.

The open-to-learning manager

While all of us encounter difficult conversations in our workplaces from time to time, many practitioners who are managers find themselves having to deal on a regular basis with difficult conversations, including dealing with complaints, giving negative feedback at appraisal interviews and discussing sensitive issues, such as sickness or family problems. While organisations may offer procedural guidance on how to deal with such situations, this still leaves many managers having to work out how to handle a multiplicity of difficult conversations, informal and formal, on an almost daily basis.

The majority of books on management that address the matter of interpersonal skills do not offer a model that takes into account the typically closed-to-learning nature of the way we handle difficulties.[12] Thus many of the suggestions offered on the management of people simply perpetuate the kind of received wisdom that reinforces closed-to-learning ways of handling difficult conversations and a closed interpretation of the social virtues.

Many books on management also fail to tackle the mismatch, described in Chapter 2, between a person's espoused theory and their theory-in-use. The value of what is sometimes sound advice is thus negated because managers convince themselves that they are operating in new ways when, in practice, their unquestioned assumptions mean that they continue to adopt a habitual, closed approach when handling their difficult conversations. Thus they may be led into believing that they have acquired useful skills whilst, in reality, their practice remains unchanged.

---

[12] This is what Argyris refers to as correcting output errors rather than looking at the source of the outputs (Argyris 1992 pp. 8-9).

This book addresses these important issues in two ways. First, by setting out the components of the open conversation approach, it offers managers a coherent, comprehensive and realistic way of dealing with the multiplicity of difficult conversations in which they become involved. By employing the principles and forms of words of the open model, and the strategy we have outlined for moving from closed to open mode (Chapter 8), managers are offered a tool for dealing effectively with the multiple and ongoing difficult conversations that are part of their responsibility.

Second, as in this chapter, the book seeks to make managers more aware of the closed interpretations of social virtues that habitually permeate the culture, and therefore the practice, of most organisations. The message is that if, as managers, we want our organisation's mission statement to have any real meaning and impact on the organisation, we need to equip the individuals within the organisation with open-to -learning skills. Unless we take these steps, mission statements will remain at the level of rhetoric.

Managers can help those they manage to become more open-to-learning by operating in ways that are consistent with open-to-learning interpretations of the social virtues. However, they first need to make sure that their own practice accords with open-to-learning interpretations of these. Otherwise their own closed practice may inadvertently legitimise the closed practice of others.

If you are a manager we suggest that you try the exercise on page 230 in order to help you examine the effects of closed and open interpretations on your own practice.

The manager as role model

Learning to deal with difficulties within an organisation must begin at the individual level (Argyris 1992 p.35). In this context, whether or not it is always recognised, managers can be powerful role models in that their influence on organisational life is usually greater than that of most other practitioners. Thus, how managers conduct their difficult conversations with others can influence how others in the organisation deal with their own difficult conversations. When managers act towards others in ways that are open-to-learning, those they manage are given a strong and positive message that open-to-learning approaches to difficulties are highly valued within their organisation.

Exercise:

Identifying any mismatches between the social virtues you espouse and how you operate in practice

If you would like to check out the possibility of any mismatch between your own espousal of an open interpretation of the social virtues and how you operate in practice, we invite you to undertake the following exercise.

Re-read each statement in Figure 11.1 (page 221), this time in the context of your own beliefs and practice as a manager.

Give each social virtue (*Respect, Support, Strength, Honesty* and *Integrity*) a rating, on a continuum from 1 to 7, to indicate how accurately it matches your belief about how a good manager should act towards others. 1 represents the most closed interpretation of a social virtue and 7 represents the most open interpretation of a social virtue, as indicted in the example below.

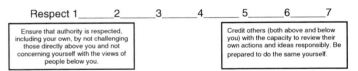

Respect 1_____2_____3_____4_____5_____6_____7

Ensure that authority is respected, including your own, by not challenging those directly above you and not concerning yourself with the views of people below you.	Credit others (both above and below you) with the capacity to review their own actions and ideas responsibly. Be prepared to do the same yourself.

Repeat the exercise but this time use the 7-point scale to indicate how often you find yourself acting in practice in closed or open ways towards others.

Note any discrepancy between your first and second set of ratings. Any discrepancy represents a potential mismatch between the extent to which you espouse the social virtue concerned, and the interpretation that affects how you will act in practice.

Consider any changes you might need to make to bring your practice more in line with the open interpretations of the social virtues.

Managers also provide a role model for the way the social virtues are put into practice. It is not enough for managers simply to espouse an open interpretation of the social virtues, through a mission statement for example. What matters is that they themselves operate in open mode with regard to the social virtues. If they operate in open mode, they will be seen, for example, to consult and listen carefully to the views of those below as well as those above them in the hierarchy *(Respect)* and to act on those views where they are likely to bring benefits. It will be noticed that they help others to review and learn from their mistakes, rather than either treating the mistake as one that does not matter or laying blame for the mistake on others *(Support)*. They will be recognised as confident enough to reveal their uncertainties *(Strength)*. They will be seen to share relevant information about particular issues with those who are most affected by them *(Honesty)*, including the reasons for decisions they have made. The fact that they are prepared to change their minds in response to reasoned argument will also be noted *(Integrity)*.

Further beneficial outcomes

As well as providing role models for the effective handling of difficult conversations, open-to-learning managers can bring about a range of other benefits within their organisations. Some examples of the likely beneficial outcomes for the workplace when managers take an open-to-learning approach to difficult conversations are illustrated in Chapters 9 and 10: open dialogue provides a basis for working relationships that can acknowledge and accommodate alternative views and within which underlying tensions can be addressed; where managers are able to give effective feedback on job competencies, poor working practices stand a better chance of being addressed and improved; the ability of managers to facilitate a co-operative approach to solving problems is likely to enhance the commitment of those they work with and to lead to solutions that enhance efficiency.

Additionally, managers who work to establish partnership in the way they handle difficult issues – the communication of unwelcome decisions, disagreements with others, their own or others' mistakes – are likely to have positive working relationships with others that enable them to exercise their management role more effectively. We would draw attention here to the research carried out by Argyris (1990) that reveals strong links between the effectiveness of senior personnel in addressing work-related difficulties and the capacity of their organisations to learn and change.

Conclusion

In this book, we have addressed a difficult, pervasive and puzzling problem: why do we all, as skilled and competent practitioners, have difficult conversations at work that are stressful and counter-productive and that impair our working relationships?

Our response to this question, based our own extensive and intensive work with practitioners, and on related theory and research, is that the problem has its roots in a way of thinking – closed-to-learning thinking – that works against us being able to handle our difficult conversations effectively. Because we are not normally able to access our closed thinking, we cannot do anything to change it. Therefore, despite our best efforts, we continue to find ourselves involved in difficult and stressful conversations.

We have argued that to deal with closed thinking and avoid its associated problems, we need to adopt an alternative model – the open-to-learning model. To achieve this we need first to identify any closed characteristics of our thinking, second to learn about the open model, and finally to make the change from closed to open. Because this is by no means easy we have also offered exercises to help us make the transition and to give us practice in thinking and acting in open-to-learning mode. We will then be in a position to make difficulties discussable and handle difficult conversations much more effectively.

Understanding the nature of closed and open-to-learning thinking, and using the closed and open models as a framework for reflecting on and learning from our practice, needs to become an integral part of our continuing professional development. When we do this, we will gain increasing fluency and proficiency in handling difficult conversations effectively.

Tough issues, and the difficult conversations that can result from trying to resolve them, will continue to come our way. However, we are confident, from our experience, that if the ideas set out in the book are taken seriously and put into practice, then, as practitioners, we will be able to manage difficult conversations more effectively whilst, at the same time, maintaining and, indeed, enhancing our relationships with those with whom we work.

Appendix A

Where the Ideas in This Book Come From

Our professional development work with practitioners

We first started to think about the ideas presented in this book in 1986. At that time Mel Myers was responsible for a national programme of professional development for educational psychologists, based at the University of Birmingham. He was looking to fill a gap in this programme – finding a way of helping psychologists to handle more effectively the many difficult conversations that their job entails. This gap was filled through the work of Michael Absolum[13] who designed a course, based on the ideas of Argyris (1974), which both authors attended. The radically new and useful learning that we experienced as a result of attending the course was the starting point for our own work in this area.

In the 20 years since that time we have developed the ideas presented in this book. We have trained and coached over 400 practitioners both as individuals and in small groups to help them become more effective in handling difficult conversations at work. These practitioners were employed in the public, private and voluntary sectors, and in further and higher education. Our work has included: workshops ranging between two and ten days' length; two years' in-house consultancy with the senior management team and sales force of an international software development company; over 40 hours of one-to-one phone coaching with senior local authority managers; and two years teaching an interpersonal skills module to MBA students, involving continuous evaluation of their progress.

In each of the above settings, practitioners worked on one or more scripts of a difficult conversation that they had experienced (as in the Key Exercise in the book). They identified closed characteristics and closed

---

[13] Michael Absolum, a psychologist from New Zealand, was in the UK on a year's exchange. He had studied at the University of Auckland with Professor Viviane Robinson who had been a student of Argyris.

forms of words in their scripts and then reworked them to produce increasingly closer approximations to open thinking and open forms of words. In total, we worked with practitioners on well over 500 such difficult conversations, analysing and reflecting on them together. It is out of this intense engagement with practitioners and their difficulties that the closed and open-to-learning models described in this book have been developed.

Of the many important findings that emerged from this work and that are incorporated into the book, we highlight just a few of particular note here. We found, for example, that almost every conversation contributed by practitioners involved one of the ten types of difficulty listed in Chapter 1. In dealing with these difficulties practitioners often felt that they had to make a choice between saying what they wanted or needed to say (and thereby risking their jobs or their relationships), or saying nothing and continuing to live with the problem. We also found that every practitioner initially approached their difficult conversation in closed mode, in that none of them questioned their assumptions or tried to make their conversations a partnership. They were extremely fluent in advocacy but almost never paired this with inquiry.

We found that, almost without exception, practitioners' use of our models helped them to improve on their initial approach to the difficult conversations they worked on.

It is from engaging in, and reflecting on, this intensive face-to-face work with practitioners that we have been able to test and refine our models to make them as accessible and useful as possible. A more detailed account of our own learning from this work is given in our article 'CPD, Lifelong Learning and Going Meta' published in the book *Continuing Professional Development: Some of Our Perspectives* (ed. J. Edge, IATEFL, 2002).

The literature

The work of the following writers has been an important springboard for our development of the closed and open conversational approaches to difficult conversations set out in this book.

- **Chris Argyris**, Professor of Education and Organisational Behaviour at Harvard, has researched and written about issues of professional effectiveness and related these to issues of organisational learning.
- **George Kelly**, Professor and Director of Clinical Psychology at the Ohio State University, psychologist and philosopher, developed an

influential theory of personhood that he terms Personal Construct Psychology. This sets out ways of making aspects of one's personal construct system available and open to inspection and modification.

- **Donald Schon**, Ford Professor of Open Studies and Education at the Massachusetts Institute of Technology, philosopher and learning theorist, has researched how practitioners learn to think and behave in the face of 'complexity, uncertainty, instability, uniqueness and value-conflict' (Schon 1983 p.39).

- **Professor Laurie Thomas** (Director) and **Professor Sheila Harri-Augstein** (Deputy Director), at the Centre for the Study of Human Learning at Brunel University, have explored ways in which individuals, teams and organisations can become more proactive and reflective in the way that they learn.

We indicate below how the work of these writers have contributed to our own thinking and practice.

Chris Argyris

(Argyris and Schon 1974), (Argyris 1982), (Argyris 1990), (Argyris 1992)

Argyris calls ways of thinking that shape people's behaviour 'theories-of-action'. He sets out two main forms of these that he terms 'Model I' and 'Model II' (Argyris and Schon 1974). Argyris' models describe people's 'governing variables' (goals) and 'action strategies' when facing difficult situations (Argyris and Schon 1974).

For Model I, the governing variables are: 'Define goals and try to achieve them', 'Maximise winning and minimise losing', 'Minimise generating or expressing negative feelings' and 'Be rational'. These give rise to the following action strategies: 'Design and manage the environment unilaterally', 'Own and control the task', 'Unilaterally protect yourself' and 'Unilaterally protect others from being hurt'. (ibid. pp. 68-72).

For Model II, the governing variables are: 'Maximise valid information', 'Maximise free and informed choice' and 'Maximise internal commitment to the choice and constant monitoring of its implementation'. These give rise to the Model II action strategies: 'Make designing and managing the environment a bilateral task', 'Make protection of self and others a joint operation' and 'Speak in directly observable categories' (make clear what is fact and what is inference) (ibid. pp. 86-90).

Argyris sees his Model I as the dominant model in determining people's actions in everyday life and one that is a source of ineffectiveness when they face embarrassment or threat (Argyris 1990 p.21). His Model II describes an alternative and far more productive way of behaving.

For us, as authors, learning to overcome the limiting effects of Argyris' Model I, and experiencing the positive impact of Model II on our own conversations, has led us, over many years, to build on Argyris' ideas through addressing the problem of difficult conversations at work. We have done this through developing the closed-to-learning and open-to-learning models set out in this book and promoting their use by practitioners.

We have drawn on most of Argryis' ideas (above), but expressed his Model I governing variables in terms of the Characteristics of our closed-to-learning model. We have developed Argyris' Model II in terms of the Principles of our open-to-learning model. In doing so we have used the term 'assumptions' to refer to any of those 'taken-for-granteds' that determine or limit a person's approach to a difficult conversation. We have also extended our account of the models to describe systematically and comprehensively how the two modes of thinking affect the forms of words we use.

In the book we refer to a number of other concepts used by Argyris:

- *Single and double loop learning.* In Argryis's work, these concepts distinguish between the limited learning and change that takes place within familiar boundaries (single loop) and the more radical learning and change that is made possible by questioning fundamental assumptions (double loop) (Argyris and Schon 1974 p.19). We refer to these concepts in dealing with closed-to-learning and open-to-learning thinking and the shift from one to the other.

- *Espoused theories and theories-in-use.* Argyris stresses the gap between people's beliefs and ideas about how to manage their lives (their 'espoused theories') and how they actually behave in practice (their 'theories-in-use') (Argyris and Schon 1974 pp.6-7). In this book, these concepts are sometimes used to represent the gap between how we like to think we deal with difficult conversations (that we are open-to-learning) and how we deal with them in practice (when as we have suggested, we are usually closed-to-learning).

- *Two-column script.* We have also found Argyris' two-column script research tool (ibid. p. 41) particularly useful for practitioners attending our courses when recording and analysing data. We use it to present the ten types of difficult conversation in Chapters 5 and 9.

The following two concepts have also contributed to our development of the closed and open models, though we do not use Argyris' terminology:

236

- *Skilled incompetence.* Argryis uses this term to refer to people's facility in behaving in ways that are maladaptive when faced with situations that he describes as embarrassing or threatening (Argyris 1990 p.21). We reflect this idea in stressing the unconscious and habitual nature of much of our behaviour, and in regarding people's management of a difficult conversation as usually reflecting their level of skill in handling the situation.

- *Ladder of inference.* Argyris describes how our (public) statements are rarely a description of data that is directly observable by others, but usually represent a conclusion we have come to after making a succession of (private) inferences from available information. He describes this succession of inferences as a 'ladder'. (Argryis 1982), with each inference in the succession being at a greater remove from the data to which it relates and from which it derives (Argyris 1992). Robinson and Lai (2006), referring to Argyris' ladder of inference, stress that:

  > 'When people realise their claims are not self-evident, and that other interpretations of the same behaviour or events are possible, they become much more open-to-learning from others.' (ibid. p.45).'

  > '...the further up the ladder one goes, the more likely it is that people will disagree about the correctness of the claim...'(ibid. p.47)

  The principles and forms of words that comprise the open-to-learning model are designed to take account of problems that can arise from the ladder of inference: awareness that the assumptions we make, and any inferences that derive from those assumptions, need to be open to question; that we need to give relevant background to what we say in order for the other person to understand how we reached our conclusions and thus be in a position to question our reasoning.

George Kelly
(Kelly 1963) (Bannister and Fransella 1971)

In his system of 'Personal Construct Psychology', Kelly holds that we all think in terms of a hierarchically organised network of 'constructs' or hypotheses about the world. He sees each of us developing our own system of constructs in order to make sense of the world around us. As it develops, our construct system becomes a filter through which we see and interpret the world, and through which we anticipate events (Kelly 1963 pp 50-53).

Like Kelly, we too put the way an individual makes sense of a situation at the heart of our work. This whole-person approach is very different from approaches based on research into discrete categories of behaviour or experience, such as non-verbal behaviour or the emotions, in order to improve corresponding areas of interpersonal communication.

Some of Kelly's other ideas have also influenced us:

- *Tight and loose constructs.* Kelly describes some of our constructs as being 'tight' in the sense that they function as certainties. Where our constructs are tight, they lock us into a particular view of the world which is impermeable and resistant to change. Other constructs are 'loose' in that they are held as provisional ideas and are open to being tested (Bannister and Fransella 1971 p. 20). The concept of tight constructs is reflected in the closed-to-learning model, where we treat our assumptions as certainties. Conversely, the concept of loose constructs is reflected in our open-to-learning model, where we treat our assumptions as hypotheses.

- *Feelings.* Kelly does not see feelings as separate from our construct system. He regards them as by- products of the way we construe the world (Bannister and Fransella 1971 pp. 21-24). This is also our rationale for incorporating the issues of feelings into our overall framework, as an integral part of relevant information exchange (Principle Three), rather than treating it as a discrete phenomenon.

Donald Schon
(Schon 1983)

Schon draws a distinction between two approaches to professional development. One is the 'technical rationality' approach where instrumental problem-solving is made rigorous by the application of scientific theory and technique. The other explores the way in which practitioners think and behave in practice. It is the latter approach that he has researched and written about most fully. In this context Schon coined the phrase 'reflective practitioner'. What he means by this is embodied in his concepts of 'reflection-on-action' and 'reflection-in-action'. These two terms describe the sort of reflection that is required if practitioners are to learn to improve their professional skills.

- *Reflection-on-action.* 'The act of reflecting-on-action enables us to spend time exploring why we acted as we did... In so doing we develop sets of questions and ideas about our activities and practice...' (Mark K. Smith, http://www.infed.org/thinkers/et-schon.htm pp. 10-11 updated version 28.6.2004).

  We have found reflection-on-action to be a useful concept. In this book we encourage the reader, especially through our key exercise, to reflect-on-action with regard to a difficult conversation in which they have participated. We hope this will enable them to identify the extent to which their own thoughts and words reveal the characteristics of closed-to-learning thinking and the constraining effect these have on the process of the conversation.

- *Reflection-in-action.* This is sometimes described as 'thinking on our feet'. 'It involves looking to our experiences, connecting with our feelings, and attending to our theories in use (see above). It entails building new understandings to inform our actions in the situation that is unfolding.' (Mark K Smith, ibid).

  Once people have understood the open-to-learning model, we ask them to practice reflection-in-action by observing and evaluating their thinking as they engage in difficult conversations and by revisiting their assumptions as the conversation develops. This enables them to engage in ongoing learning every time they are involved in a difficult conversation.

Laurie Thomas and Sheila Harri-Augstein

(Harri-Augstein, E.S. and Thomas, L.F.1985) (Harri-Augstein, E.S. and Webb, I.M.1995)

A number of concepts developed by Thomas and Harri-Augstein, at the Centre for the Study of Human Learning at Brunel University, have been very useful in developing our two models and in formulating suggestions as to how these models might be put into practice.

- *Personal learning myths.* Thomas and Harri-Augstein define these as unquestioned beliefs – positive or negative – about our abilities. As such they represent a class of assumptions that can severely limit personal endeavour and attainment unless they are made explicit and tested (Harri-Augstein and Webb 1995).

  Our own treatment of assumptions in both the closed and open-to-learning models parallels this idea, in that we draw attention to the

239

restrictive effect of unquestioned assumptions on our ability to deal effectively with difficult conversations.

- *Robotic behaviour.* Thomas and Harri-Augstein term a behaviour 'robotic' when we perform a skill in a way that is not under our control. Even a performance that we might see as creative (for instance in art or music) can be robotic if we cannot explain in detail what we did and therefore cannot improve on it (ibid).

  The concept of robotic behaviour is reflected in our closed-to-learning model where behaviour is habitual and unconscious.

- *Self-organised learning.* The self-organised learner accepts responsibility for their own learning rather than being dependent on the initiatives and directives of others, is aware of how they learn and of the dynamic nature of the learning process (ibid. p.10-11). Self-organised learners become adept at developing tools to facilitate their own learning.

  In this book we encourage the reader to become a self-organised learner by carrying out the exercises supplied in each chapter. These draw on the readers' own experiences of difficult conversations and supply the basis for ongoing experimentation and learning.

- *Phases in the process of improving a skill.* Thomas and Harri-Augstein propose a model of skills improvement that identifies a number of phases in people's learning. In Phase One people are 'unconsciously incompetent' in that they start off being unaware of the inadequacy of their level of skill. In Phase Two they become 'consciously incompetent', in that they have now become aware of their skill deficit but have not yet learnt how to remedy it – this can be an uncomfortable phase to be in, and the one in which help and encouragement is most likely to be needed. In Phase Three they become 'consciously competent'. They now know what they are trying to do when they engage in the skill, and in a way that enables them to give themselves feedback on their own performance and therefore learn from it.

  In the context of this book, Phase One would represent the likely starting point of the practitioners who read this book, in that before reading the book they are unaware that they might need to learn new skills in order to improve their difficult conversations. Phase Two reflects an understanding of how the closed-to-learning way in which they habitually approach difficult conversations contributes to the difficulties they experience. However they do not yet know an alternative, open-to-learning approach. Phase Three is made possible by practitioners' understanding of the open-to-learning approach. Once they understand this approach they can use it as a basis for reflection 'on' and 'in' their practice (cf. Schon, above) and therefore for their ongoing learning. The high level of consciousness that characterises Stage Three is always essential if we are to remain open-to-learning and avoid falling back into closed mode in our difficult conversations.

Appendix B

Instructions for Key Exercise

Step 1:
Recording one of your own difficult conversations

Using the form on page 245 as a guide, describe briefly *the setting* within which you have had a difficult conversation with another person that left you feeling dissatisfied, either because of their response or because of your own performance. If you are unable to think of a work example, either try the reminiscence exercise (Chapter 1 page 29) or choose one from another situation.

Describe briefly *what it was* about the conversation that you found *difficult*.

In the right-hand column, write down, as in the script for a play, the conversation that you had with the other person. Just script the bit of the conversation from where it started to 'go wrong', rather than scripting the whole of what could be a lengthy conversation. You may not remember this exactly but capture it as accurately as you can. Aim for between one and two sides of A4.

In the left-hand column, write any concurrent *thoughts* and *feelings* you had as you talked. Describe these as fully as possible. In particular, make sure that you include any *thoughts* that, for whatever reason, *you did not put into words* (we shall consider these thoughts in Step 2). Write your thoughts and feelings as you go, rather than adding them after you have completed the right-hand 'words' column. Continue on a separate sheet if necessary.

Briefly *evaluate the conversation*, commenting on *how effective* your handling of the conversation had been and *how you felt at the end of it*.

Form for writing your script of a difficult conversation

Setting for the conversation:	
My difficulty with the conversation:	

My thoughts	**My words and (name of the other person)'s words**

Evaluation of how well I handled the conversation

My feelings at the end of the conversation

The layout of your work should look something like this (in the example **B** refers to the other person).

Setting for the conversation:

B and I manage different departments in the same organisation. We'd arranged a meeting to discuss how we could avoid duplicating our efforts. When we got to the room we were supposed to be meeting in we found it was occupied and there were no other suitable rooms free.

My difficulty with the conversation:

B wouldn't acknowledge that it was her responsibility to book the room.

My thoughts	My words and (name of the other person)'s words
Oh no. The room's taken. I assumed **B** would have booked it..... after all, the room's in her building	
	Me. Didn't you book the room?
I'm so annoyed. I can't do everything. I remember now she was helpless the last time we had an interdepartmental meeting. Why doesn't she take some initiatives!	**B.** I thought you were doing it
	Me. No. I had enough to do preparing the agenda and sending the papers out.. The room's in your building. All you had to do was walk down the corridor.
	B. I never said I'd do it. After all you were the one who wanted the meeting.
What does that mean!	
etc.	etc.

Evaluation of how well I handled the conversation

I couldn't get **B** to acknowledge that she should have booked the room. We had an argument. What did become clear to me was that B wasn't really interested in the meeting anyway.

My feelings at the end of the conversation

I was glad I found out about **B**'s feelings before I wasted more time on setting up another meeting, but I felt annoyed at her attitude and we didn't exactly part on the best of terms.

Step 2:
Evaluating your thoughts in terms of the closed-to-learning model

Evaluating your thoughts

Take a close look at the left-hand column of your transcript, the one containing your thoughts. See if you can identify any of the three Characteristics of closed-to-learning thinking that we have described in this chapter. Mark any instances you find of each of any of the characteristics on the script as you go, making notes of any observations. The following notes can be used as prompts.

Characteristic One (We do not question our assumptions)

Are you making any unquestioned assumptions? Underline any unquestioned assumptions – especially any that prevented you from making a concern discussable or otherwise led to the conversation being ineffective. In the process you may also become aware of unquestioned assumptions that you failed to identify when you did the exercise. If this is the case, write them in the margin.

Characteristic Two (We do not promote partnership)

To what extent did you feel as though you were trying to manage the conversation single-handedly or independently of the other person? Make use of the section on Characteristic Two in Chapter 3 to identify any ways in which your thinking during the conversation failed to take into account the need to check out the other person's thoughts and wishes.

Characteristic Three (We do not promote the exchange of all relevant information)

In your thoughts column, underline any information which could have given the other person a better understanding of your position but which, for whatever reason, you withheld from them. Consider whether any of your assumptions prevented you from communicating this information. Make use of the section on Characteristic Three in Chapter 3 (Characteristic Three) to remind yourself of the sort of relevant information you may not have thought necessary to give or to get.

Step 3:
Evaluating your words in terms of the closed-to-learning model

Take a look at the right hand column of your transcript, the column containing your words and those of the other person. Looking only at your words, see if you can identify any of the following:

Advocacy that lacks transparency

- Look for, and underline, any examples of statements of opinion (advocacy) you made without making it clear that you were expressing a personal view. Try to imagine the extent to which such statements may have come over as inflexible or dogmatic or difficult for the other person to question or challenge.

- Look for, and underline, any statements of opinion (advocacy) you made without giving enough evidence for your opinion (or the reasoning behind it) to enable the other person to understand how you came to your conclusion. As above, consider the extent to which such statements may have come over as inflexible or dogmatic.

Inquiry that is not genuine

- Mark any instances when you asked a 'question' (inquiry) which came over as lacking in genuine information-seeking intent. Consider whether such a question might have made it difficult for the other person to reply without appearing confrontational.

Advocacy without inquiry

* Look for any examples of 'advocacy without inquiry'. Underline and label these examples. Can you find any places where a failure to inquire might have allowed the other person to avoid responding to what you said and/or made it more difficult for them to let you know what they really thought about your views?

Inquiry without advocacy

* Look for any examples of 'inquiry without advocacy'? Underline and label them. Can you see how asking a question (inquiry) without saying why you were asking it (lack of advocacy) might have made it more difficult for the other person to give you an informed response?

    Examine whether your actual reasons for asking the question were ones that you would have felt quite able to give (had you thought to do so), or whether the reasons were ones that you preferred not to disclose.

    Consider whether the conversation might have taken a different turn if you had explained the reason you asked your question.

    Once you have worked through this exercise consider how any of the effects of closed-to-learning thinking on advocacy and inquiry may have contributed to the difficulty of the conversation.

~~~~~~~~~~~~~~~

Finally, you might, for your own learning, consider to what extent do you think your way of handling this conversation is typical of your everyday approach to your conversations at work.

Step 4:
Revising your thoughts in terms of the open-to-learning model

The purpose of Steps 4 and 5 is to put together the first set of words you would use, were you to replay the conversation in open-to-learning mode.

Follow the instructions on the form below which will help you to ensure your thoughts are open-to-learning (Step 4).

Principle One: Question any relevant assumptions	
List any assumption(s) you underlined in your script that influenced how you handled the conversation.	How might you deal with these assumptions so that they do not influence your approach in a negative way? (See Principle One in Chapter 6.) Write down your ideas *without, at this stage, worrying about what words you might use to the other person.*

Principle Two: Promote partnership in the conversation

Select from the suggestions for implementing Principle Two in Chapter 6, one or two that you could use to promote partnership in this conversation. Write down your ideas *without, at this stage, worrying about what actual words you might use to the other person.*

Principle Three: Promote the exchange of all relevant information

Select from the suggestions for implementing Principle Three in Chapter 6, one or two which might be useful in promoting the exchange of valid and relevant information. Note any specific information you might want to give and get. Write down your ideas *without, at this stage, worrying about what actual words you might use to the other person.*

Step 5:
Revising your words in terms of the open-to-learning model

With your open-to-learning thoughts in mind, write a new opening set of words (or first response) for your conversation with the other person. Ensure that advocacy is transparent and inquiry genuine, and that any advocacy is paired with inquiry and any inquiry is paired with advocacy. Keep this speech short – you can say more later, as appropriate.

My revised words

Had you been in a position to use your new thinking and your new words at the time of the original conversation do you think that you would have been able to handle the conversation more effectively?

References

Absolum, M. (1985). *Behaving for the future: Developing processes for democratic relating.* Unpublished dissertation: University of Aukland.

Absolum, M. (2006). *Clarity in the classroom.* Hodder Education, Auckland.

Argyris, C. (1982). *Reasoning, learning and action: Individual and organisational.* Jossey-Bass, San Fransisco-London.

Argyris, C. (1990). *Overcoming organisational defences: Facilitating organisational learning.* Allyn & Bacon, Needham Heights, MA.

Argyris, C. (1992). *On organizational learning.* Blackwell Publishers, Cambridge Mass.

Argyris, C & Schon, D.A. (1974). *Theory in practice: Increasing professional effectiveness.* Classic Paperback, Jossey-Bass, San Francisco.

Bannister, D. and Fransella F. (1986). *Inquiring man: The psychology of personal constructs (3rd. edition).* Croom Helm, Beckenham.

Harri-Augstein, E. S. and Thomas, L. F, (1985). *Self-organised learning: Foundations of a conversational science for psychology.* Routledge and Keegan Paul, London.

Harri-Augstein, E. S. and Webb, I. M. (1995). *Learning to change: A resource for trainers, managers and learners based on self-organised learning.* McGraw-Hill, New York.

Kelly, G. (1963). *A theory of personality: The psychology of personal constructs.* Norton, New York-London.

Myers, M. and Clark, S. (2002). *CPD, lifelong learning and going meta.* In Edge J. (ed.) *Continuing professional development: Some of our perspectives.* IATEFL, Whitstable.

Robinson, V. and Lai, M.K. (2006). *Practitioner research for educators: A guide to improving classrooms and schools.* Corwin Press, Thousand Oaks.

Schon, D. A. (1983). *The reflective practitioner: How professionals think in action* (paperback edition). Ashgate, Aldershot.

otl@reflectiveprocess.co.uk. Address for emailing comments on the book.

www.reflectiveprocess.co.uk. Website with information about availability of personal instruction and practice.

Glossary

[Starred items: these definitions reflect our particular application of a widely-used term.]

A and B
Terminology used to indicate the two participants in the annotated conversations in Chapters 5, 9 and 10. *A* represents the person who is the focus of the annotations and *B* the other person in the conversation.

Advocacy
Statement(s) a person makes that convey the way they sees things, their concerns, wishes, views, reasoning, or feelings.

Alert & cue
Being aware of negative feelings in the course of a conversation (alert) and using this awareness as a prompt (cue) to remember the three principles of open-to-learning thinking.

Assumption
Any idea, interpretation, inference or belief that, for the purposes of discussion, planning and action, a person takes to be true.

Characteristics of closed-to-learning thinking
Characteristic One. We do not question our assumptions.
Characteristic Two. We do not promote partnership.
Characteristic Three. We do not promote the exchange of all relevant information.

Closed advocacy
Advocacy that comes from, and reflects, closed-to-learning thinking.
- **Advocacy is not transparent**
  Advocacy that does not include enough information for the listener to be able to assess the validity of what is being said.
- **Advocacy without inquiry**
  Advocacy that is not accompanied by an inquiry to check the other person's response to that advocacy.

Closed conversation
An approach to conversations that is based on the closed-to-learning model.

Closed inquiry
Inquiry that comes from, and reflects, closed-to-learning thinking.
- **Inquiry is not genuine**
  Inquiry that does not constitute a genuine request for information.
- **Inquiry without advocacy**
  Questions that do not give the other person enough information about the speaker's position to enable the listener to make an informed response.

Closed-to-learning model
A description of the characteristics of closed-to-learning thinking and the related forms of words that characterise an ineffective approach to difficult conversations.

Closed-to-learning thinking
The type of thinking that leads one to handle difficult conversations ineffectively.

Difficult conversation
A conversation that is hard to handle and gives rise to negative feelings.

Discussable (as in 'making concerns discussable')
Concerns can be raised, and talked about in a way that is acceptable to both participants.

Double loop learning*
Learning that is made possible by questioning those assumptions that would otherwise limit a person's thinking.

Effective conversation
A conversation in which difficulties are made discussable and where there are beneficial outcomes.

Espoused theories/values
The beliefs or values that people profess. *See also* Theories/Values-in-use.

Forms of words
Ways of formulating the words used in a conversation that result from, and express, closed or open-to-learning thinking.

Ineffective conversation
A conversation in which difficulties are not made discussable and where there are adverse outcomes.

Information exchange
The two-way communication of the concerns, wishes, views, reasoning or feelings of the people involved in a conversation.

Inquiry
Questions that request information about the way the other person sees things, their concerns, wishes, views, reasoning or feelings.

Open advocacy
Advocacy that comes from, and expresses, open-to-learning thinking.
- **Advocacy is transparent**
  Advocacy includes enough information for the listener to be able to assess the validity of what is being said.
- **Advocacy with inquiry**
  Advocacy that is paired with inquiry requesting the other person's response to that advocacy.

Open conversation
An approach to conversations that is based on the open-to-learning model.

Open inquiry
Inquiry that comes from, and expresses, closed-to-learning thinking.
- **Inquiry is genuine**
  Inquiry constitutes a genuine request for information.
- **Inquiry with advocacy**
  Inquiry that is paired with information explaining why the question is being asked.

Open-to-learning model
A description of principles of open-to-learning thinking and the related forms of words that make up an effective approach to difficult conversations.

Open-to-learning thinking
The type of thinking that enables those who adopt it to handle difficult conversations effectively.

Partnership
A way of addressing a difficulty that sees the conversation as an opportunity for finding jointly acceptable ways forward rather than as something to be managed alone.

Principles of open-to-learning thinking
Principle One: Question any relevant assumptions.
Principle Two: Promote partnership.
Principle Three: Promote the exchange of all relevant information.

Reflection-in-action*
Reflecting on one's own thinking and forms of words whilst in the process of having a conversation.

Reflection-on-action*
Reflecting on one's own thinking and forms of words either before or after a conversation.

Round
A short section of conversation consisting of *B*'s words, *A*'s thoughts and *A*'s words.

Single loop learning*
Learning that is limited by our failure to question one's assumptions.

Social virtues
Values that, within a particular culture, are widely held to be desirable.

Theories/Values-in-use
The beliefs or values that people find themselves actually using in practice. *See also* Espoused theories/values.

Index